SHARI FROST

Rethinking
INTERVENTION

SUPPORTING STRUGGLING READERS *and* WRITERS *in* GRADES 3–6 CLASSROOMS

CHOICELITERACY

Choice Literacy, P.O. Box 790, Holden, Maine 04429
www.choiceliteracy.com

Copyright © 2014 by Shari Frost

Every effort has been made to contact copyright holders for per-
mission to reproduce borrowed material. We regret any over-
sights that may have occurred and will be pleased to rectify them
in subsequent reprints of the work.

Library of Congress Cataloging in Publication Data Pending

ISBN 978-1-60155-046-0

Cover and interior design by Martha Drury
Manufactured in the United States of America

19 18 17 16 15 14   10 9 8 7 6 5 4 3 2 1

To Art

CONTENTS

ACKNOWLEDGMENTS

I've been taught much by my teachers and even more by my colleagues. But more than by all of them, I've been taught by my students.
                    —Rabbi Chanina, Babylonian Talmud, Tractate Taanit

For more than a dozen years, I've been fortunate to be "taught" by wonderful literacy coaches, interventionists, classroom teachers, and their students. All of the stories in *Rethinking Intervention* emerge from their classrooms.

I would like to thank the coaches and interventionists with whom I've had the privilege of enjoying one-to-one relationships: Evelyn Acevedo-Nolfi, Javier Arriola, Lara Beaver-Medina, Jay Brandon, Julie Buzza, Kay Connley, Jeanne Hunter, Luanne Kowalke, Jennifer LaMar, Mary Loss, Amanda Luna, Christine Michalik, Paula Stafford, Denise Thul, and Wanda Williams-Sims. I admire the wisdom, dedication, commitment, and drive that you repeatedly exhibit as you support teachers in providing the best possible literacy instruction for their students.

I am also very appreciative of two different sets of classroom teachers. The first set of teachers allowed me to follow their literacy coaches into their classrooms and sometimes stay for a very long time: Kathleen Kennedy, Michelle Martinez, Kim Moore, Rita Nicky, Mindy Rench, Alexis Schmitz, and Erica Simon. The second set of teachers provided me with the opportunity to work with them directly in their classroom settings: Chantay Baker, Laura Bigby, Loretta Edwards, Sharon Morgan, and Kiwanna Phillips.

Thank you, Camille Blachowicz, for choosing me to develop and direct the Literacy Coaching Collaborative at National-Louis University. I will always remember and cherish your confidence in me. To the coaches in the Literacy Coaching Collaborative, thank you for sharing your stories, struggles, triumphs, and insights. To my partner in crime, Roberta Buhle, much love and thanks.

Finally, I would like to thank my editor and friend Brenda Power. Your encouragement, support, patience, and just the right amount of pressure were exactly what I needed to tell my story.

MONICA:
AN INTERVENTION STORY

Monica, a sixth grader, was the subject of a recent intervention conference at a public school in the suburbs of a large Midwestern city. Such intervention conferences are held quarterly to monitor the progress of students receiving intervention services. Intervention services are well established at Monica's school. However, the quarterly meetings are a recent phenomenon. The conference was attended by Monica's classroom teacher as well as all the other sixth-grade teachers, the interventionist, the literacy coach, and the case manager. Monica's current level of literacy achievement is two years below grade-level expectations. She has received intervention services since she was in second grade.

The interventionist reported that Monica is a cooperative and hardworking student. She shared the results of a recently administered Developmental Reading Assessment and assessment records from the intervention kit used in the program. The assessments revealed that Monica is making steady progress. The interventionist also shared some of the workbook pages that Monica had completed that week, highlighting how neatly and thoroughly they were done.

The classroom teacher shared the results of the annual state reading test that was administered at the end of the previous school year. From among possible classifications labeled Advanced, Proficient, Below, and Academic Warning, Monica was deemed to be reading at the Below level. The teacher reported that Monica always does a good job on homework assignments, but she often fails to successfully complete in-class assignments. Monica needs to have directions repeated, and she must periodically be redirected back to the assignment. The teacher said that although Monica appears to be attentive when the class is working in content-area textbooks, she doesn't seem to understand what she is reading. She cannot correctly answer factual questions about a chapter that the class has just read in the textbook.

After hearing the teacher's and the interventionist's reports, the case manager suggested that perhaps the intervention is not working and something else should be considered. The interventionist responded in alarm, "But Monica has always been in intervention."

The case manager is probably right. Something is indeed not working. Monica is in her fourth year of receiving intervention services, but she is still reading two years below grade level. The assessment data show that she is making progress, but it is not sufficient to close the gap between Monica and her grade-level peers. Monica's story is not unique. For many students, intervention becomes almost a life sentence. Why is this happening? Everyone seems to be trying so hard.

Monica's school recognizes the need to provide extra support for struggling students. They have allocated funds in their budget for an intervention program. They have designated a sunny, attractively furnished room for intervention classes. They have hired staff to teach the intervention classes. They have purchased special intervention texts and materials. They have developed a schedule that allows students to take some time away from the regular instructional program to receive intervention services. Now they have instituted progress-monitoring meetings to discuss the progress of students receiving intervention services.

Monica's intervention teacher appears to be a hardworking, conscientious professional. She has meticulously maintained records of Monica's assessments over the years and graphed the results on a chart. She has a well-worn teacher's edition of the intervention program, which is tabbed with sticky notes and has writing in the margins. She also maintains a folder containing the workbook pages that Monica has completed under her supervision. Judging by the bulkiness of the folder, Monica has been completing two to three workbook pages each day. Clearly, Monica has been busy working during the intervention period.

Monica's teacher also seems to be hardworking and conscientious. Her classroom is orderly, well managed, and well organized. She has an up-to-date record book noting the students' grades on assignments and tests. She also has a lesson-plan binder with current lessons. A schedule is written on the whiteboard and strictly adhered to. All of the students have color-coded folders for each subject. The teacher rings chimes when it is time for a new activity. Monica and her classmates quickly and quietly transition from one activity to another. The students are attentive during the lessons and work diligently on their written assignments.

Monica's parents are clearly making an effort to support her. The teachers' records reveal that they have never missed a parent-teacher conference. The records also include a reading log, which Monica's parents sign upon the completion of each book that she has read. Monica has a good attendance record and comes to school every day with completed, accurately done homework assignments. In combination with her struggles to complete her classroom assignments, this suggests that she is getting a lot of help from her parents with homework.

Then there is Monica. She is trying. Her teachers describe her as "cooperative and hardworking." She doesn't "forget" her homework assignments at school, even though she knows that they will be frustratingly hard for her to complete and that her parents will undoubtedly have to intervene to get her through them. She takes the time to complete all of those workbook pages, and she even takes the additional time to ensure that they are completed in a neat fashion. She is not disruptive in class.

Yes, everyone is trying. But even though everyone is "doing their part," Monica is still reading two years below grade level. It is time to rethink the way we provide intervention instruction to struggling learners. Monica might have made sufficient progress for the intervention to be discontinued at some point during its four-year duration if her school had managed to overcome some of the pitfalls of providing intervention instruction.

IDENTIFYING THE PITFALLS OF INTERVENTION

PITFALL 1: THE INTERVENTION TEACHER

The decision to provide intervention services to a student is seldom made lightly. There has to be sufficient evidence that the student cannot be successful with regular classroom instruction alone. There is often a history of failure, such as low report card grades and test scores or even retention. The classroom teacher has tried to help by placing the student in a small group with other struggling students to better target instruction to meet his needs. Parents have been notified, and ideally they have become more vigilant about supervising homework, increasing the opportunities to read at home, and prepping the student for upcoming tests. Only after these efforts have failed to yield the desired results is the decision made for the student to receive intervention services. Often, some of the impetus for this decision comes from a parent or teacher who is strongly and actively advocating for the student.

So what kind of teacher do you think would best be able to provide successful intervention instruction to these students who have not succeeded with regular classroom instruction? Wouldn't you think that the teacher would have a little something extra above and beyond the training and experience of the run-of-the-mill classroom teacher? In fact, the intervention instructor should be an experienced teacher who has a track record of successful teaching. He or she should have specialized training—more than a bachelor's degree in elementary education. He or she should probably hold an advanced degree in literacy from a graduate program that included coursework in teaching struggling readers and preferably also a practicum in a supervised clinical setting, providing the teacher with the opportunity to work with actual struggling readers with the support of expert university instructors.

Unfortunately, this is not always the case. Frequently, the students who need the most skilled, highly trained teachers are taught by anyone, from volunteers and paraprofessionals to teachers who have no specialized training at all. Why? Many school administrations believe that this is an economically sound decision. A skilled and highly trained literacy professional is likely to be at the top of the salary scale for teachers. Why pay those higher salaries for literacy professionals when two to three paraprofessionals can be hired for the same price or, with luck, volunteers will do the job for free?

The knowledge base for volunteers and paraprofessionals can range from certified, experienced teachers to someone with absolutely no training at all. Some school districts are so attractive to preservice teachers that they are willing to accept a paraprofessional position there, hoping it will lead to an eventual teaching position in the district. Even though these paraprofessionals are certified teachers, they are usually inexperienced. Sometimes, a school is lucky enough to have a retired teacher serve as a volunteer. Even in that case, it is important to assess whether the retired teacher has the requisite skill and knowledge to work successfully with struggling readers.

Then there are the paraprofessionals and volunteers who have no formal teacher training. Sometimes the schools offer some training—but even the most extensive of such training programs entail no more than 12 hours of instruction spread out over several days. It is impossible for such a crash course to provide adequate preparation for success with the same struggling readers who have been unsuccessful even with fully trained classroom teachers. Some schools might even have a teacher or literacy coach supervise the volunteers and paraprofessionals. Supervisors periodically observe lessons, give feedback, answer questions, and try to clear up confusions. Though such supervisors are a step in the right direction, success is still highly unlikely with paraprofessionals and volunteers who have inadequate training or no training at all. And, unfortunately, the situation is often even worse; it is not at all uncommon for a volunteer or paraprofessional to be handed a box of materials, pointed to a work area, and told to work through the lessons to the best of his or her abilities.

Yes, a school can initially "save" thousands of dollars in salaries, but the overwhelming majority of the students receiving intervention will continue to require intervention services in future years. Initially, less money has been spent, but has any really been saved?

PITFALL 2: ALL-INCLUSIVE PACKAGED INTERVENTION PROGRAM

In recent years, there has been an absolute explosion of materials available to teach struggling readers. Almost every published reading textbook program includes an intervention component. Trade-book publishers, professional-book publishers, and leveled-book publishers are all touting their all-inclusive intervention kits. These intervention kits include all sorts of goodies such as leveled books, decodable books, workbooks, word cards, magnetic letters, whiteboards, software, tests, games, and manipulatives. They all make big promises and incredible claims. For some reason, school administrators believe these claims. Maybe it is because the boxes are so slick, shiny, and attractive. Maybe it is because they are so expensive—most of them cost thousands of dollars. If it costs so much, it has to be good, right? Schools buy these materials and hope that this time they have finally found the answer. Besides the missed opportunity to help the struggling readers, just think of all the wonderful books that could have been bought with all of that money!

Let's open the pretty box and examine what is inside. Does the box contain sufficient instructional-level texts for the intervention student to be engaged in actual reading for 75 percent of the intervention period? Would the students actually want to read the books in the box? Does the box contain lessons that include a meaningful writing component? Do the lessons engage students in continuous writing—more than a single word, a phrase, or a sentence? Do the lessons encourage ongoing dynamic assessment rather than having instruction screech to a grinding halt for a weekly testing day? Are the lessons flexible enough to meet the needs of diverse students and learning styles?

Or are the lessons fixed and rigid? Do the lessons come with a script that tells the teacher exactly what to say? Are the lessons dominated by word study activities that take up as much as 40 percent of the intervention period? Are the included texts phonetically regular, giving students many opportunities to apply sound/symbol knowledge but little opportunity to gain proficiency in using the other cuing systems of reading? Do the texts have controlled, stilted, and unnatural-sounding language? Do students ever get a chance to read authentic texts—the kind they will need to read in the real world? Is a significant portion of the intervention time devoted to assessment, as much as one period each week? Are there entire lessons focused on a single "comprehension subskill," such as identifying the main idea or drawing conclusions?

Packaged intervention programs give schools false hope. With their explicit, scripted lessons, they propagate the big myth that anyone at all can successfully teach struggling students to read. Their cookbook, step-by-step approach seems so simple; if you follow the prescribed lessons as written, the students will improve. Some programs even suggest that paraprofessionals and nonprofessionals can (or should) do the teaching.

To avoid giving an even worse impression of these programs than they deserve, I should point out that most of them are not totally devoid of usefulness; indeed, some of the intervention kits on the market contain some very nice components. However, the most important component of a successful intervention program is a knowledgeable and responsive teacher who can make informed decisions based on students' reading and writing behaviors. A responsive teacher knows how to use the materials to best meet the needs of the students. The teacher drives the instruction in response to the students, not the materials, and cannot be locked into a predetermined next step that doesn't depend on how the students react to the current step. Unfortunately, a skilled teacher doesn't come with the kit.

PITFALL 3: MINIMIZING THE ROLE OF THE CLASSROOM TEACHER

Everyone breathes a sigh of relief when a struggling student finally begins to receive intervention services. We are hopeful that this new venture will soon have the student on the right path to success in schooling. Unfortunately, some teachers have gotten the wrong idea about intervention. They may believe that when a student receives intervention services, the intervention teacher is responsible for all of that student's reading instruction.

How can that be? The average school day is six to seven hours long. The average intervention lesson is 30 to 45 minutes long. Intervention students work with their classroom teachers for the bulk of the school day. The intervention services are only supplemental. Yes, the lessons are more intense and targeted to the students' specific needs, but they are still less than 10 percent of the school day.

There also needs to be high-quality, differentiated reading instruction in the regular classroom. Intervention students need to have opportunities to read independent-level texts for enjoyment and fluency-building, instructional-level texts with the teacher's guidance to gain proficiency in reading and exposure to grade-level texts. The last of these causes some degree of frustration for most intervention students—but grade-level texts contain the grade-level curriculum and content that intervention students still need to learn, even if they can't access the texts without some adaptations.

The classroom teacher has a critical role in teaching reading to students who receive intervention services. Intervention students learn specific strategies during the intervention lessons to help themselves when they read and write. Where will they do much of that reading and writing? They'll do a lot of it in their regular classroom. The classroom teacher provides intervention students with the opportunities to apply what they learn during their intervention lessons to the independent- and instructional-level reading that they do in their regular classroom.

Having reading instruction restricted to the intervention classroom is a little like learning to drive exclusively on a practice range. The practice range is free from the distractions of other drivers and pedestrians while the student learns the basics of how to operate the vehicle. The intervention teacher provides those intensive, targeted "practice range" lessons in the safety of the intervention classroom away from the distractions of a full classroom. The ultimate goal of the practice range is to get the drivers out on the road. The role of the classroom teacher is to make sure that intervention students are indeed out on the road and do not remain forever on the practice range.

Yes, intervention students need to have reading instruction in their regular classrooms, too. They need to work with their classroom peers in literature discussion groups, strategy study, guided reading groups, and writing in response to reading. The classroom teacher makes adjustments to ensure their full participation.

PITFALL 4: THE INTERVENTION CURRICULUM

The goal of all intervention instruction is for the student to be successful in the regular classroom. If you want students to do well in regular classroom instruction, then the intervention curriculum has to be aligned with the classroom curriculum.

A common and frequent misconception is that the intervention curriculum should be skills-based. Universal and diagnostic assessments have revealed that intervention students are "deficient" in certain print processing and comprehension skills. Therefore, the intervention curriculum focuses on teaching and building proficiency in those isolated word-solving and comprehension skills. There are many cases of students who become quite successful in the intervention class but continue to struggle with the regular curriculum.

PITFALL 5: GOALS FOR INTERVENTION STUDENTS

It is pretty exciting when things finally start to click for students who have struggled with reading and writing. Although we celebrate every step forward, we can't take our eye off the ultimate goal: to close the gap between intervention students and their grade-level peers. Anything less than achieving that goal is setting up the students for a possible return trip to intervention services. Think of it as abandoning your diet when you are down a pants size but still not at a healthy weight.

Retaining students in intervention classes year after year without closing the gap is not acceptable. Action must be taken to avoid repeating past mistakes and dooming our school systems to large numbers of Monicas.

This book will not address the "how-tos" of delivering intervention instruction. This topic has gotten a lot of attention in recent years. There are several good books out there for those purposes, listed below. Instead, in this book, I look specifically at an aspect of the intervention process that has received little or no attention—the role of classroom instruction and the classroom teacher. I look at instructional practices that teachers can use to support intervention students in whole-group and small-group instruction. I describe some effective in-class interventions. Finally, I talk about how classroom teachers and intervention teachers can team up to attain the goal of closing the gap between intervention students and their grade-level peers.

Recommended Professional Resources for Intervention Instruction

Allington, R. L. (2011). *What really matters for struggling readers: Designing research-based programs.* New York: Allyn and Bacon.

Dorn, L. J., and Soffos, C. (2012). *Interventions that work: A comprehensive intervention model for preventing reading failures in grades K–3.* Boston: Pearson.

Fountas, I., and Pinnell, G. S. (2008). *When readers struggle: Teaching that works.* Portsmouth, NH: Heinemann.

Lyons, C. A. (2003). *Teaching struggling readers: How to use brain-based research to maximize learning.* Portsmouth, NH: Heinemann.

Paratore, J. R., and McCormack, R. L. (2011). *After early intervention, then what? Teaching struggling readers in grades 3 and beyond.* Newark, DE: International Reading Association.

WHOLE-CLASS INSTRUCTIONAL PRACTICES THAT SUPPORT STRUGGLING READERS

Allie is a sixth-grade teacher. She recently told me about a team meeting that she attended to address the specific instructional needs of Justin, one of her students. The meeting was attended by the school psychologist, the social worker, resource teachers, Justin's parents, and his teachers, including Allie. One of the recommendations given to the teachers to address their concerns about Justin's apparent inability to remain focused on a task was to redirect him every 10 minutes!

Allie left the meeting feeling very frustrated. How was she supposed to redirect Justin every 10 minutes? Set a timer? Would she have to limit her minilessons, her work with small groups, and individual conferences to nine minutes each? How would

Justin ever learn to be self-regulated if his teachers assumed total responsibility for keeping him on task? How would Justin feel about being singled out so frequently?

Some suggestions made to help teachers with struggling learners are just not practical, or even realistic. A team that is focused on an individual student sometimes seems to forget that there are 20 to 30 other students in the class who also need some of the teacher's time and attention. One of the greatest challenges in teaching is determining and meeting the instructional needs of all students in the class, even when the class is made up of students with a wide range of abilities. In particular, teachers must find ways to address the specific needs of individual students while continuing to work with the whole class.

The instructional practices recommended in this section are suitable for the whole class. They are presented here specifically with respect to struggling readers, but they can undoubtedly be used with minor modifications for struggling learners in other areas as well. They are highly supportive of the struggling readers in the class without neglecting the students who are meeting and exceeding grade-level expectations. These practices do not require any specialized materials, equipment, or training.

WHOLE-CLASS INSTRUCTIONAL PRACTICE 1: A WORKSHOP FRAMEWORK

Allie's student, Justin, didn't really have a problem staying focused on a task. He loved to draw. In fact, he could draw without too much distraction for hours on end. He had piles of notebooks filled with detailed drawings of fantastical creatures and settings. This demonstrated that he was indeed capable of staying focused on a task. What he couldn't do was stay focused while he attempted to read his sixth-grade textbooks. They were much too difficult for him. The workshop framework is a way to keep students like Justin meaningfully engaged during literacy instruction.

Workshop isn't really an instructional *practice*; it is an instructional *framework*. The workshop framework organizes instruction in a manner that maximizes opportunities for students to work toward individual goals at their independent and instructional levels. The workshop concept emerged in elementary and secondary classrooms during the 1980s.

The workshop framework has three major components: the minilesson, work time, and share time. The teacher traditionally begins the workshop with a short, focused lesson (minilesson) based on the overall needs of the class and/or the required curriculum.

Then, there is work time—the students read and/or write independently or in groups. While students are busy with their reading or writing, the teacher conducts individual conferences and works with small groups of students.

Workshop ends with share time. It is an opportunity to revisit and reinforce the concepts presented in the minilesson and to celebrate learning. Teachers and students reconvene to reflect on the work done and the insights gained. The teacher might invite a student to talk about the way(s) he has applied what was taught during the minilesson. Another student might be asked to read aloud an interesting passage from the book she is reading or from her personal response journal. Someone else might share what he has learned about himself as a reader. Or a group of students might report on the processes that they used during group time. The students or groups chosen for any of these activities are not selected randomly or haphazardly; the teacher specifically chooses them based on her interactions with them during individual conferences and small-group work. Sometimes, the teacher will also briefly sum up the minilesson concepts during share time.

What makes workshop the ideal framework for Justin and other struggling readers? First of all, it provides time for students to actually read. Instead of completing worksheets and workbook pages, or building dioramas and making posters, students are reading. We can all agree that volume of reading is critical to reading improvement, especially for struggling readers (Allington, 2011). Workshop is structured to allow for an increased volume of reading.

It is well documented that proficient readers read significantly more than struggling readers (Cunningham and Stanovich, 1998). Because proficient readers read more, they further increase their reading proficiency and vocabulary, and they gain more insights into how literate language works. In other words, the more they read, they better they get at reading. This phenomenon only widens the achievement gap between proficient readers and struggling readers. Most struggling readers are not reading outside of school. This is understandable. Nobody wants to spend a lot of time doing something that they don't do very well. Although we continue to work on ways to encourage and support reading outside the school setting, in-school reading time remains immensely important; in fact, its value is almost impossible to overestimate.

In workshop, Justin does not have to struggle with a sixth-grade-level reading anthology; students are encouraged to read books at their independent-reading levels. An independent-level book is one that a student can read with 97–100 percent accuracy. Allie assists Justin in selecting books that he would be interested in reading, increasing the likelihood that he will actually read them. Look at it as an equation: independent level + topics interesting to student = more time spent reading. Workshop is the perfect environment to get Justin there.

Another reason that the workshop framework is especially supportive of students like Justin is the time it allocates for teachers to work with small groups and conduct individual reading conferences. The most effective instruction that Justin can receive is one-to-one instruction. A reading conference is an individualized, custom minilesson for a student. A conference can be used to identify and assist with obstacles to comprehension. In addition, Allie can use conference time to monitor Justin's book choices to ensure that she is ready to make book recommendations that keep the reading going. Teachers are mindful of books that students enjoy and stock the classroom library with their favorites. Not all conferences are full fledged and formal; some of them are mini-conferences in which the teacher simply touches base to make sure that all is well.

Allie might work with Justin in a small group of struggling readers several times a week. Small-group lessons are developed to meet the specific instructional needs of struggling readers. Any one (or more) of the following can be the focus of a productive lesson for a small group of struggling readers:

- The teacher can provide follow-up on the minilesson, giving the struggling readers additional guided practice. It is often helpful for these students to apply what was taught in the minilesson to the book that they are currently reading.

- Students can practice a strategy that will help them comprehend texts, such as inferring.
- Students can practice a skill that the teacher might have noticed them struggling with, such as pronoun antecedents.
- The teacher can guide readers through a book at the students' instructional level. An instructional-level book is a book that students can read with about 95 percent accuracy. That makes it a good book for helping students learn how to problem-solve. There is virtually no problem solving in an independent-level text.

Not all small groups are led by the teacher. In the workshop framework, students can get together in small groups to discuss a particular book. These groups, called book clubs, are often heterogeneous, giving struggling readers a chance to work with on-level peers. Allie carefully selects specific books and students for a book club to ensure a successful experience for Justin and the other struggling readers.

The typical alternatives to a workshop framework are a whole-class novel or whole-class reading from a grade-level reading textbook. These alternatives are problematic for struggling readers because they cannot read the book; its level is too high for them. The time they spend on lessons from a grade-level reading textbook or a whole-class novel is lost instructional time that they simply cannot afford to lose.

Teachers attempt to accommodate struggling readers in these instructional formats by assigning them a reading partner (which entails potential social problems) or allowing them to listen to an audio recording of the book or textbook. Obtaining an audio recording is usually not problematic; almost all reading textbook packages include audio recordings of the selections, and many novels are available in audio format. However, these accommodations for struggling readers are of limited benefit. Specifically, they are helpful only in the sense that they enable participation in the discussion about the current novel or reading selection, and in the case of a reading partner, even this benefit can disappear if the reading partner is not assigned with care. Unfortunately, struggling readers aided by either an audio recording or a reading partner are not reading during reading time, and they will never become more proficient readers if they don't read. These accommodations fail to address the main instructional need of struggling readers; they are analogous to a medical treatment that addresses symptoms but does nothing about the underlying cause of the disease.

In grades three through six, a workshop session can range from 60 to 90 minutes. What might a 60–90 minute reading workshop look like for Justin?

Minilesson	10–15 minutes
Small-group work	15–20 minutes
Independent reading	15–20 minutes
Conference	1–5 minutes
Writing	10–15 minutes
Share time	10–15 minutes

Justin, like many struggling readers, lacks the stamina to read for more than 20 minutes in a sitting. Workshop is the perfect instructional environment for building stamina, and it also provides other useful and productive ways for him to use his time until he can actually "get lost in a book" for 30 to 45 minutes at a stretch. Ideally, each struggling reader should spend the maximum amount of time doing independent reading that is compatible with his level of stamina, and the workshop framework has the flexibility to allow for independent reading time to increase as more stamina is developed.

WHOLE-CLASS INSTRUCTIONAL PRACTICE 2: INTERACTIVE READ-ALOUD AND SHARED READING

Do you remember using a kickboard when you were learning how to swim? The kickboard kept you afloat and allowed you to concentrate on your kicking. You didn't have to think about what you were doing with your arms or worry about your breathing. Interactive read-aloud and shared reading are the "kickboards" of reading instruction. The teacher either does all of the reading, as in interactive read-aloud, or highly scaffolds the reading of the text, as in shared reading, so that the students can devote all of their energy and concentration to under-standing the text's content or learning the strategy that is being taught.

INTERACTIVE READ-ALOUD

Interactive read-aloud is a deliberate and explicit instructional reading strategy. In a carefully planned and prepared lesson, the teacher models and teaches vocabulary, fluency, comprehension strategies, and sometimes even content-specific information. The teacher makes his or her thinking visible, or transparent, through think-alouds. Stopping points are designated throughout the book, enabling the teacher to highlight vocabulary while providing opportunities for the students to get some guided practice with comprehension strategies and to discuss the text with each other and the teacher. The teacher selects a book that will best support the lesson's focus.

Sara reflected on her last individual conference with Tyler, one of the struggling readers in her third-grade class. He was reading one of those 70-page chapter books written at a late-second- to early-third-grade reading level. Tyler was excited about the book because he recognized that it was similar to the books that the on-level readers were reading. In the conference, she listened to him read most of the first chapter of *Donovan's Word Jar* (DeGross, 1998). Although his reading was accurate, he was definitely missing the inferences. For example, the text said, "On days when his mom packed raw broccoli and cauliflower in his lunch, Donovan forgot to eat them." Sara asked, "What's going on here?" Tyler said, "He was probably talking to his friends and forgot to eat all of his lunch."

Tyler wasn't the only student struggling with inference. Most of Sara's third graders were accurate readers. Their literal comprehension was good. However, if something was not explicitly stated in the text, many of them completely missed the point. In other words, Sara's conference with Tyler was far from unique, and she found herself frequently coaching individual students and small groups on inference. She concluded that it was necessary to address this comprehension issue as a whole group, so she decided to do an interactive read-aloud with the book *Dear Mrs. LaRue: Letters from Obedience School* (Teague, 2002). This book is written at a third-grade reading level, so most of Sara's students would be able to read it without any external support, and the interactive read-aloud would help make it more accessible to Tyler and the other students who were not yet reading at that level. Also, there are three other books featuring the same main character, which could help induce students who have enjoyed this book to keep reading.

Sara prepared this lesson by reading through the book several times; she needed to review the content, determine good stopping points, and practice delivering a good read-aloud performance. She decided how much of the lesson would be modeled and how much would be devoted to shared and guided practice. She affixed tabs on pages where she would stop. She affixed a sticky note to the inside cover with her plan. She used an LCD projector to project the pages that she wanted the students to see in print for guided practice. Finally, she got a sheet of chart paper for an anchor chart.

Sara gathered her students in the whole-group meeting area. After showing the book's cover and reading aloud the title and the author's name, she started by thinking aloud about the title page. She pointed out that the dog was straining on the leash and pulling Mrs. LaRue into the path of an approaching bus and that the package Mrs. LaRue had been carrying was in the air, presumably because she had dropped it while trying to hold on to the leash. Sara proceeded by reading the first page, which consisted of a newspaper story reporting that Ike, Mrs. LaRue's dog, was being sent away to obedience school. Sara commented that she was not surprised by this development based on the example of Ike's behavior depicted in the title page illustration.

The remainder of the story is told in the form of letters written by Ike to Mrs. LaRue. Only Ike's letters appear in print. The reader must infer, based on each of Ike's letters, what Mrs. LaRue must have written in response to his previous letter. Sara modeled inferring the contents of Mrs. LaRue's first three letters, written before Ike's letters of October 1, 2, and 3, respectively. She supported her inferences by going back into the text for evidence.

When she got to Ike's letter of October 4, she projected the page onto a screen. Collaboratively, the students inferred what Mrs. LaRue must have written in her previous letter. Then she had the students "turn and talk" about what Mrs. LaRue must have written right after that based on Ike's next response, written on October 6. Tyler and Jeremy had an animated conversation about "the help" Ike gave to Mrs. LaRue when she crossed the street. When Sara asked for volunteers to share with the whole group what they had discussed with their respective partners,

Tyler was happy to talk about these insights. At the end of the book, Sara and her students discussed why Mark Teague had made some illustrations in color and some in grayscale. They talked about what they could infer from Teague's use of color.

Sara ended the lesson by noting that sometimes an author will come right out and tell us everything that is happening in a story, but sometimes we have to use what we know (schema) and look for clues in the text to fill in some missing details. The group started an anchor chart on inferring using some examples from the book.

A good read-aloud book offers many instructional opportunities. Sara can revisit this book to explicitly teach vocabulary, using words such as *misconceptions, severely, retrieve,* and *endure.* She can point out how Mark Teague's word choices help us understand Ike's character—a tip for her students' writing. She might invite the students to actually write some of Mrs. LaRue's letters to Ike or do a character analysis of Ike. *Dear Mrs. LaRue: Letters from Obedience School* has obvious inferences. The next interactive read-aloud might be with a book in which the inferences are more subtle.

How did Tyler benefit from this lesson? Since Sara did the reading, he was able to concentrate on understanding the concept of making inferences. Sara used gradual release: first modeling, then engaging the students in a shared experience, and finally providing some guided practice. This lesson structure was supportive of Tyler and the other struggling readers. He was able to observe the teacher inferring and hear her thinking throughout the process. Then he got to try it along with the teacher. He was never called out or put on the spot. When guided practice was provided, it was in pairs, a format that enabled Tyler to get support from Jeremy, a respected peer. Of course, this will not be the final lesson on inferences. There will be minilessons, small-group work, and follow-up in individual conferences. The students have had this anchor experience, complete with a chart that they can refer to when they need support.

The following week, Sara convened a small mixed-ability group containing both struggling readers and on-level readers to read one of the other books about Ike. Tyler is a member of that group. He will benefit from having peer models, and he will also be able to draw upon his experience and knowledge of the main character from the read-aloud book.

SHARED READING

I know what you're thinking. Kindergartners are sitting "criss-cross applesauce" on a colorful ABC rug in front of a big-book version of *Brown Bear, Brown Bear* (Martin, 1967) as the teacher points to words using a pointer with a sparkly star on the end. Right? Yes, that is shared reading. But shared reading is also a classroom of sixth graders reading and discussing the Gettysburg Address. Shared reading is an instructional approach in which the teacher and the students collaborate to read a text while the teacher explicitly models the strategies and skills of proficient readers. In kindergarten, that means modeling skills such as directionality or voice-print matching. In sixth grade, it means modeling strategies such as using text structure to predict the flow of information or synthesizing. Shared reading in the intermediate and upper grades has been shown to be an effective instructional strategy (Allen, 2000, Brown, 2004; Fisher, Frey, & Lapp, 2008). Allen describes shared reading as "the heart of reading instruction" (p. 58).

Amy was one of the struggling readers in Rhonda's fifth-grade class. Rhonda reread Amy's story "The Payless Princess," which was about a girl who was being ostracized by her classmates because she wore shoes purchased at Payless Shoe Store. The story was action driven; it went quickly from one event to the next. The characters were not very well developed; Amy did a lot of telling instead of showing. There were sentences such as "She was very sad," instead of scenes that were created to show the character's sadness. Rhonda was thrilled that Amy had jumped into the fiction-writing craze that was sweeping through the class's writing workshop. It meant that she was more engaged in writing and was writing more.

As is often the case, the challenge in writing also showed up in Amy's reading. Amy seemed to focus on the action when she read. She could easily tell what had happened, but she often missed the subtleties that contributed to a rich story. In literature discussion groups and individual conferences, Rhonda had noticed that Amy seemed to be flying through or maybe even skipping the rich descriptions that authors provided. Amy wasn't the only student who tended to skip the descriptions. For example, when one of the groups had been discussing *Because of Winn Dixie* (DiCamillo, 2009), they had barely mentioned Gloria Dump's tree during the discussion. Rhonda wanted Amy and the rest of her students to realize why these types of descriptions would help give them a better understanding of the story.

Successful shared-reading lessons begin with careful planning. A lesson focus needs to be determined. An appropriate text for teaching the focus skill or strategy needs to be selected, and a decision has to be made on how to make the text visible to all of the students. What can you teach with shared reading? Fisher et al. (2008) learned that intermediate- and upper-grade teachers were most likely to use shared reading to explicitly teach comprehension strategies such as activating background, inferring, summarizing, predicting, clarifying, questioning, visualizing, monitoring, synthesizing, evaluating, and connecting. Shared reading can also be used to teach vocabulary, writer's craft, text structures, and text features. Shared reading can even be used to teach content-area concepts and math problem solving.

After the lesson's focus has been determined, begin the search for those texts that will best help your students achieve the lesson's goals. A variety of texts can be used for shared reading. Use passages from novels, poetry, essays, picture books, speeches, newspaper articles—almost anything. It is important that the text fit the lesson's purpose. If you want to teach activating background knowledge, you might use a newspaper article. If you want to teach visualizing, you might want to use poetry.

Shared reading works best with shorter texts. Remember that the purpose of shared reading is instructional; it is used to demonstrate a skill or a strategy. One of the common misuses of shared reading is using it to read an entire novel. It is almost impossible to pace the reading of an entire novel appropriately for a classroom full of students; any given pace will inevitably be too slow for some students and too fast for others. The book selected will almost always be too easy for some students, making shared reading inappropriate, and too hard for others. Can you imagine how tedious it would be to read aloud and read along for an entire novel? You can be sure that many students would check out after the first few days.

Rhonda decided to do a shared reading using the book *Seedfolks* (Fleischman, 2004) with her fifth-grade students. The shared-reading lessons would help to meet important instructional needs for both the students' reading and the students' writing. Fleischman's careful word choices help readers visualize the scenes that he creates, and Rhonda planned to emphasize this aspect of the book to help the students learn to appreciate the value of the descriptions that many of them had heretofore been just skimming or even completely ignoring. Once students develop an awareness of these visualizing techniques in their reading, they will be ready to incorporate similar techniques into their writing as well; thus, Rhonda's shared-reading choice was also designed to serve as a mentor text for "show, don't tell" as a writing skill for her students.

In addition, Rhonda wanted to expand her students' reading repertoire. The girls were gobbling up the Allie Finkle (Cabot) and Melanie Martin (Weston) books, and the boys were fighting over the Wimpy Kid (Kinney) and Percy Jackson (Riordan) books in the classroom library. *Seedfolks* is a realistic fiction novel with a gritty, urban setting. It is a little heavier than the light fiction and fantasy that was dominating the students' reading logs. It is written at a late-fourth-grade reading level, so many of Rhonda's students are capable of reading it with no external support. *Seedfolks* is made up of individual vignettes. Each vignette is self-contained, so a reader can choose some or all of them. Since it is only 67 pages long, maybe even Amy and some of the other struggling readers would be willing to take it on.

After the text is selected for a shared reading, decide how to make it visible to the students. This can be accomplished by

- projecting it onto a screen with an LCD projector,
- displaying it on the smartboard,

- making an enlarged copy,
- writing the text on chart paper or the whiteboard, or
- providing students with their own copies of the text, although I do not recommend this (see below).

There are even some big books that were specifically written to be used with students in the intermediate and upper grades. But a problem with many of those big books is that the print is often too small for all of the students to see in a whole-group setting. If the students can't see the text, the book is useless. Rhonda photocopied and enlarged the pages that she had chosen for the class to read, and she planned to project them onto a screen with an LCD projector.

Students, especially struggling readers, need to actually be looking at the text during a shared-reading lesson. Many teachers opt to give each student his own copy of the text before the lesson, but this is not recommended. Although you'll eventually want everyone to have a copy of the book, it is better for one enlarged text to be shared during the whole-group lesson because it is difficult to monitor whether students' eyes are on the text when they each have their own copy. By all means, pass out individual copies to all interested students after the shared-reading lesson is over.

To teach a shared-reading lesson, begin by explaining the purpose of the lesson to the students. Tell them what they're going to do and why they'll be doing it. Direct the students' attention to the text. Always start a shared reading by reading aloud at least the first few sentences. This enables you to set the tone, cadence, and pace. Some teachers pause (oral cloze) when the students are to join in. Develop your own plan for signaling the students that it is time to orally read along.

Rhonda was now ready for the lesson. She told her students that they were going to read a chapter called "Curtis" from the book *Seedfolks* (Fleischman, 2004). She said that they would be reading the chapter to see how authors develop characters and help readers visualize the characters. She told the students to listen to the words and to try to visualize how Curtis looks. If they saw Curtis walking down the street, would they recognize him? She asked them to think about what kind of person Curtis is and how Fleischman was able to develop his character in only three and a half pages.

Rhonda read the first three sentences with "attitude and bravado." Then she signaled the students to join in. They finished reading the first paragraph together, mimicking the style that Rhonda had modeled, after which they temporarily broke away from the text to talk about Curtis's appearance. Rhonda pointed out that Fleischman never uses words such as *muscles* or *muscular*, even though those words were being used to describe Curtis during the class discussion. She asked her students to point out how we know that Curtis is muscular. She also asked what kind of person Curtis seems to be. The students responded, "He's a show-off. He's 'stuck on himself.' He thinks he's all that." Rhonda instructed them to find the words in the text that had led them to those conclusions about Curtis.

Rhonda read the next paragraph and had the students join her in reading the following paragraph. After stopping for a while to identify the problem in the story and to predict how Curtis might solve the problem, they read the rest of the page to confirm their predictions. In the final two pages, the students took note of Curtis's actions and decisions. Were these actions and decisions consistent with their initial description of Curtis as vain and a show-off? After the reading, they discussed whether Lateesha would forgive Curtis. Finally, they talked about the author's craft: Fleischman's opener, word choices, transitions, showing instead of telling. They talked about how the tomatoes looked at various stages of growth, how the garden looked, and how Lateesha looked as she peeked out the window at the garden. Rhonda invited the students to draw Curtis, Lateesha at the window, or the tomatoes in their reader response journals.

Amy and her classmates were eager to get back to their writing after the lesson. In the following days, when Rhonda met with groups and individuals, the students talked about what they visualized in their reading and made a better effort to "show" rather than "tell" in their writing. Amy asked Rhonda if she could read the rest of *Seedfolks*. Rhonda gave her a copy, producing a parade of students who wanted to know if she had another copy—including some of the other struggling readers.

How does shared reading support Amy and other struggling readers? It allows them to focus on the strategy or the skill instead of on the text that they might find too intimidating. It gives them access to texts that they cannot read on their own but that are within their zone of proximal development. It exposes them to grade-level texts. It provides the scaffold necessary for some of them to actually attempt to read the text in a teacher-directed group or maybe even a student-led group.

Another important benefit of shared reading is that it builds community. Both struggling readers and capable readers experience the same story together. Teachers and students are partners in constructing meaning from a text. It helps build confidence and helps struggling readers see themselves as successful readers.

WHOLE-CLASS INSTRUCTIONAL PRACTICE 3: SHARED WRITING

Belinda was feeling rather discouraged. She had just finished reading drafts of her students' argument writing. After several minilessons and conferences, most of her fourth graders were still not supporting their position statements, especially the struggling learners. Perhaps the problem was the topics. Only a few of the students had generated their own topics. The rest had relied on the cliché topics that Belinda had provided as examples, such as school uniforms, no homework, and later bedtimes—nothing that they were strongly passionate about. Feeling resigned, Belinda planned the minilesson for the next day's writing workshop based on what she had noticed in the latest drafts.

The next morning, as Belinda was rereading her uninspiring minilesson plan, her students exploded into the classroom. They were all talking at once, every one of them terribly upset. "What happened?" Belinda inquired. Olivia said, "At a school board meeting last night, they voted to stop Halloween celebrations in school. No parties, no parades, no costumes!" That was the most language that Belinda had heard from Olivia all year. Olivia was one of the struggling learners in the class. She was new to the community and hadn't made any friends yet. Olivia's coping strategy of choice was to attempt invisibility. She was very quiet. She never volunteered in class, always sat slumped in her seat, and didn't interact with the other students when she worked in groups. She mumbled through writing conferences, and Belinda had to strain to hear her monosyllabic responses. She wrote in the tiniest handwriting that Belinda had ever seen.

"It's not fair," the students wailed. Belinda seized the moment. She instructed the students to put their jackets away and gather on the carpet. There, the students took turns talking about how they felt about the school board's decision. They related how much they had looked forward to Halloween since the first day of school. Some of the students' mothers were already in the process of making their costumes. Others talked about window-shopping at the costume store in the mall. They shared memories of Halloween celebrations from as far back as kindergarten.

Belinda asked if anyone knew why the school board had ended the Halloween celebrations. Once again, Olivia spoke up. She and her mother had attended the meeting to request an additional bus stop closer to Olivia's house, so she had heard the whole debate. Olivia reported that the school board was concerned about

- loss of instructional time because of celebrations,
- children eating too much candy and junk food,
- exclusion of children who do not celebrate Halloween because of religious restrictions, and
- children feeling bad because they couldn't afford fancy costumes.

Belinda quickly jotted down the reasons on the whiteboard. She was surprised to hear such a well-ordered and articulate description of the issues from Olivia, who clearly had been listening closely at the meeting and had successfully retained the details in her memory overnight.

Belinda told her students that the school board had presented a good argument to the community that Halloween should not be celebrated in school. They had given four specific and well-founded reasons for their position, which they embraced with passion. Their reasons showed that they cared about the students. They wanted the students to be healthy and to spend their time in school learning, and they didn't want any students to feel left out.

Belinda suggested that the class write to the school board in an effort to present the positive aspects of Halloween celebrations in school. The students loved the idea. Belinda loved it, too. Here was an authentic reason for using argument writing. She could cash in on the students' passion to help them understand the importance of providing support for a position. Rather than having the students write individual letters, she'd do a shared-writing letter to demonstrate how to construct an argumentative essay. The school board was more likely to read a single letter than 25 of them. In addition, by means of the collaborative process, they could finish the letter in a few days; writing individual letters would take at least a week.

SHARED WRITING—AN OVERVIEW

Shared writing is an instructional strategy in which the teacher and the students collaborate in writing a message. The teacher acts as the scribe and mediator. Shared writing is appropriate for students from kindergarten to middle school (Routman, 2004). Depending on its purpose, the length of the message can vary greatly, from as short as a few sentences to as long as a complete, multi-page story or report. Individual shared-writing sessions are short, ranging from 5 to 15 minutes, so it sometimes takes multiple sessions to complete a piece.

Shared writing entails a high level of teacher support, but the level of student control is also significant. Shared writing is in the "we do" portion of the continuum of gradual release of responsibility. In the hands of a skillful teacher, shared writing uniquely enables students of widely differing ability levels to all work within their zones of proximal development.

Shared-writing lessons provide a myriad of benefits for struggling learners. More specifically, shared writing supports struggling learners by

- actively involving them in the creation of a meaningful text that they might not be able to create independently;
- helping to solidify and further develop their store of known words for reading and writing;
- reinforcing the conventions of written language through meaningful engagement rather than through isolated drill and skill practice;
- reinforcing word-solving strategies through active engagement;
- demonstrating the writing process (prewriting, drafting, revision, editing, and publishing) through active engagement;
- developing additional insights into how texts are crafted;
- engaging them in using literary language;
- generating text that all students can read; and
- serving as a catalyst for independent writing.

The shared-writing message in Belinda's class took the form of a letter, but shared writing can also be used effectively for a message in any written format, including

- a written response to reading,
- a learning log entry,
- a summary,
- a report,
- documentation of a class experience,
- an original story, and
- a variation or innovation on a story.

Shared writing's versatility is by no means limited to its format; it also works well with any topic or genre. In short, anything that can be written can be written using shared writing.

Belinda used shared writing to reinforce instruction in a specific writing genre—argument writing. It is also an excellent way to demonstrate and provide guided practice for a new writing genre. Before you expect students to write in the new genre, it is a good idea to provide a shared-writing experience. Perhaps Belinda's students would not have struggled as much with argumentative essays if they had engaged in a shared-writing experience early in the process.

SHARED WRITING IN ACTION

In most cases, the first step in a shared-writing activity is for the students to gather together near the place where the shared message will be recorded. At this gathering, the teacher and the students negotiate about what they are going to write (topic, format, genre, and so on). It works well to have the students sit on the floor at the chosen place; a rug makes this more comfortable. Belinda chose the whole-class meeting area for the shared-writing lesson, but in her case it was unnecessary to gather the entire class there because the topic and format had already been agreed upon.

After the initial gathering, the students are divided into triads, and time is provided for them to engage in some prewriting discussion of their ideas for the shared-writing message before the whole group takes on the task. Because Belinda was able to skip the initial gathering, she began the entire activity at the triad stage. Doing this before the whole-class discussion serves several purposes.

- It ensures that there is an audience for all ideas.
- It allows students to rehearse what they want to say.
- It provides a safer environment for students who are reluctant to speak up in the whole group.
- It enables each student to have input into the shared message even though the message will not be long enough to contain a separate sentence for each student.

The students who worked with Olivia welcomed her into the group and valued the insights that she had to share. For the first time, Olivia actively participated in a group activity.

After the prewriting talk, most shared-writing groups reconvene on the rug, but Belinda's class convened there for the first time. They generated a web to capture the groups' ideas. They decided that their letter would have three parts:

- thanking the school board for caring about their health, education, and happiness;
- rebutting the school board's arguments for ending Halloween celebrations; and
- presenting their own arguments for continuing Halloween celebrations.

Belinda pointed out that they had engaged in prewriting and stressed the importance of thinking and planning before writing—the better the planning, the better the writing. As she was saying this, Belinda guiltily recalled the measly amount of time that had been devoted to the argumentative-essay drafts that were now sitting on her desk.

Before they ended the first day's shared-writing session, they worked on an opening sentence. Belinda thought it was important to have at least the start of the letter posted to maintain the students' enthusiasm. It was also an opportunity to stress the importance of openers to capture the reader's attention. Together with the entire class, she listened to the students' ideas—and, as a group, they selected the following opening sentence for the letter.

Dear School Board Members,
We were devastated to learn that a Grinch has stolen our
Halloween celebration.

The idea of the "Grinch that stole Halloween" had been Olivia's. Belinda made a mental note of Olivia's familiarity with Dr. Seuss books.

It was now up to Belinda to physically record the chosen sentence (to be followed eventually by the rest of the shared message), and she grabbed a sheet of poster-sized sticky note for that purpose. A variety of media can be used to record a shared-writing message, including a sheet of chart paper, a chalkboard, a whiteboard, a smartboard, or word processing software with an LCD projector. If you use a chalkboard or whiteboard for drafting the message, you'll hve to transfer it to paper. Revisions and edits are easily made with the high-tech options (smartboard or word processor/projector); if you take the low-tech route, you'll need a marker for writing and correction tape to make revisions or edits. No matter what medium is used, it is crucial for all students to be able to see the writing; this entails, among other things, making certain that the writing is large enough. After the opening sentence was recorded, the shared-writing session ended for the day.

Over the next three days, the class worked on writing the text of the letter. This entailed approximately equal amounts of talking, writing, and reading. When the group agreed on a sentence, Belinda would first say it out loud and then write it down, saying each word again as she wrote it. Then the group would reread the sentence. If someone thought that the sentence should be revised, they would need to say how it should be revised and explain why the revision would improve the letter. After each sentence was finalized, with or without revisions, they went back and reread all the written text before going on to the next sentence.

Shared writing requires "in the moment" decision making. Belinda's emerging knowledge of her students' strengths and limitations helped her make good decisions. The shared-writing lesson moved along at a brisk pace to maintain a high level of student interest and engagement. Several "teachable moments" emerged during the writing of the letter, but to maintain sufficient continuity, Belinda didn't interrupt the process to address each of them; she planned to revisit the letter for additional instructional opportunities in future minilessons and conferences. The letter was an authentic writing experience, not just an exercise. All the students got to sign the letter, and it was sent to the school board office.

This story has a happy ending; there were three positive outcomes. First, the school board decided to allow the Halloween celebrations to take place for the current year and appointed a committee to study the issue for upcoming years. Apparently, there was an enormous outcry from the community. The school board was besieged with letters, phone calls, and emails of protest. Belinda's fourth graders believed that it was their letter that brought about the decision. Belinda was happy to allow them to believe in the power of their writing.

Next, the fourth graders went on to write much better argumentative essays. Many of them abandoned their previous efforts and started anew. They increased the amount of time spent on prewriting by brainstorming topics and scouring the local newspapers and the Internet for ideas. They talked to each other about issues that were really important to them, and they made progress in planning and writing improved essays.

Finally, Belinda learned that shared writing is a powerful instructional practice for supporting and including struggling learners. Since Belinda was "holding the pen," Olivia was free to actively participate in composing the message; she did not have to struggle with spelling and other writing conventions. Freed from dealing with the written word, Olivia came out of her shell. Although she had trouble reading and writing, she apparently had no difficulty with spoken language. Shared writing provided Olivia with the opportunity to watch spoken language appear before her in print. Two of the sentences that Olivia had contributed ended up in the final copy of the letter. Because of the multiple rereadings of the letter, Olivia was able to read it without assistance.

Belinda started a Dr. Seuss book club, which Olivia joined. The club members read books such as *The Sneetches* and *The Lorax* that were more advanced than the beginning books such as *The Cat in the Hat*. They wrote argumentative essays on topics that emerged from these books, such as the importance of recycling. The use of rhyme in the Seuss books helped Belinda address some the word-solving problems that Olivia was experiencing.

WHOLE-CLASS INSTRUCTIONAL PRACTICE 4: USING A THEME TO LINK BOOKS

One of the challenges of teaching is finding the right books and materials to address specific instructional goals. Once a teacher has found the perfect book to help his students understand a literary element, practice a comprehension strategy, or tie into a thematic unit, it becomes part of his permanent teaching repertoire. However, one problem with these "perfect books" is that they are often not accessible to the struggling readers in the class. This is yet another way that these students might be missing out on instructional opportunities. A solution to this problem is to continue the search even after the perfect book has been found. Find two or three more perfect books, so that all the students in your class have access to an appropriate text.

Peter, a sixth-grade teacher, looks forward to National Poetry Month all year long. It is in April, right after a couple of weeks of grueling standardized testing. Then Peter and his students spend a glorious month enjoying poetry. He can feel the tension in the classroom dissipate as his students jump headfirst into his great collection of poetry books, Friday poetry read-alouds, and wonderful poetry-writing activities. In past years, one of the highlights of this unit has been the whole-class reading of the book *Bronx Masquerade* (Grimes, 2002). This edgy book, featuring prose and poetry interspersed with each other, really resonates with his urban students.

However, after the latest reading conference with Jamal, Peter had to admit that *Bronx Masquerade* would be much too difficult for him. Although the book is written at a fifth-grade reading level—a full year below the expected reading level of the class—Jamal would take one look at the text-dense pages (the ones that don't contain a poem) and throw his hands up in defeat without even trying.

Peter mentioned the problem to Marla, the school's literacy coach. She suggested that they meet after school to explore some possible solutions. The first thing that Marla showed Peter was his class profile. Although Jamal, who was reading at a late-second-grade level, was sitting there at the bottom of the list, there were a few other students not too far above him—students reading at the third- and fourth-grade levels. Marla suggested that perhaps *Bronx Masquerade* was too difficult for those students, too. Peter bristled at the thought. He had used the book for the past three or four years and it had always worked, or at least he thought it had. Marla thought that maybe Peter should offer other book options, so that these students could read a book that was more within their reach. She handed him a stack of books that she thought might work with the unit.

Peter was disappointed. He had hoped that Marla would give him some suggestions for helping Jamal read *Bronx Masquerade*, using some kind of reading specialist's trick that he didn't know about. The last thing he wanted to do was hand Jamal a second-grade book—not that he would read it or even be caught dead with it in his possession. A few weeks earlier, a whole stack of leveled books from Jamal's reading intervention class had been discovered stuffed into the back of his locker. Besides, Peter didn't think that there could possibly be another book out there that told a great story, had compelling poetry, and reflected his students' lives. He took the stack of books that Marla offered him, but he wasn't optimistic.

Peter was wrong. Not only was there another book that told a great story, had wonderful poems, and had characters his students could relate to—but there were two of them! Just as in *Bronx Masquerade*, the characters in these books were students learning about poetry in school and using poetry to help them cope with issues in their lives. One of the books, *Locomotion* (Woodson, 2004) was written at a reading level about a year lower than *Bronx Masquerade*. It wasn't quite as edgy, but the main character was an urban boy who was in foster care. A few families in Peter's school community took in foster children. This year, two of his students lived with those families. The last book, *Love That Dog* (Creech, 2001) was a lot easier and not edgy at all. However, Peter still liked the book and thought that some of his students would, too.

He didn't want to just hand Jamal the easiest book, so he went back to Marla for ideas. She suggested that Peter first give book talks for all three books, then give the students a chance to peruse the books, and finally, ask the students to write their names on a slip of paper along with the titles of their first and second choices. That was exactly what Peter did. He realized that several of his students would benefit most from *Love That Dog*, but he worried that they would be dissuaded from choosing it because of the stigma induced by its easy level. He used the book talk as an opportunity to give *Love That Dog* a very hard sell, and he was surprised and gratified to see that a larger-than-expected number of students had bought into his pitch and selected it as their first choice—including, as he had hoped, Jamal. So Peter formed groups, and they got to work.

Peter taught the same poetry minilessons for *Locomotion* and *Love That Dog* that he had always taught for *Bronx Masquerade*, including poetic forms, literary devices, literary language, and line breaks. He also taught the same literature and comprehension minilessons, such as characterization, visualizing, flashback, prediction, and making connections. The minilessons always sent the students back to their books to find examples. In writing workshop, they imitated the poems, like Jack did in *Love That Dog*. They also tried out concrete poetry, haiku, occasional poems, and free verse. They collected vivid verbs in their writing notebooks.

Peter met with small groups three times a week, one day for each of the books. Each book group had 8 to 12 students in it, and he extended an open invitation to all readers of the book who wished to meet with him. Usually, five or six students would come to the table. The other students read in pairs, in triads, or individually. He had individual conferences twice a week. In these conferences, he kept tabs on everyone's progress with the books. Sometimes he would recommend that a student attend the next small-group session or change reading partners. Some of the students ended up reading all three of the books. It made Peter uncomfortably aware that some of his students from past years had very likely finished *Bronx Masquerade* weeks before his lessons had ended. This year's class had other reading options.

Having students share across books made the lessons even more powerful. The class made a chart (shown on the next page) to keep track of the comparisons.

The poetry unit was a huge success. Peter's students were never more engaged and on task during reading. As in past years, they had Open Mike Fridays, just like the characters in *Bronx Masquerade*, to read aloud favorite and original poems. This year, they also designated one of the classroom's bulletin boards for posting their original poems, à la Miss Stretchberry in *Love That Dog*. Peter also invited the students to start poetry notebooks, like Lonnie in *Locomotion*. The notebooks started out as a place for the students to copy their favorite poems, but for many of the students it soon evolved into a place for both their imitated and original poetry.

Peter had to expand his poetry-book collection to include some of the works of the poets mentioned in the two new books. Also, in past years' units on *Bronx Masquerade*, he had not included any of Nikki Grimes's poetry books in his collection because most of them were in picture-book format. After all, it was sixth grade, and he was sure that his students would turn up their noses at them. This year, he took a risk and brought a few of them in. His students loved them! He raided the school and public libraries for all of Grimes's picture poetry books that were available. These books were perfect for Jamal and the other struggling readers. There was no stigma in reading them, because

	Bronx Masquerade	Locomotion	Love That Dog
Main character	Tyrone and his classmates	Lonnie Collins Motion	Jack
Main character's problem	Overcoming challenges of poverty and adolescence	Parents died, and separated from sister	Dog killed in auto accident
The teacher	Mr. Ward	Mrs. Marcus	Miss Stretchberry
Types of poetry learned	free verse concrete poetry rap	haiku sonnet rap free verse occasional poems	concrete poetry lyric poetry narrative poetry free verse
Poets studied	Langston Hughes Nikki Grimes Claude McKay Amiri Baraka James Weldon Johnson Countee Cullen Pedro Pietri	Langston Hughes Jacqueline Woodson Richard Wright	William Carlos Williams Walter Dean Meyers Robert Frost William Blake Valerie Worth Arnold Adoff S. C. Riggs
How they shared their poems	Open Mike Fridays	Poetry notebooks	Bulletin board
How poetry helped	Gave them hope for the future	Gave him a way to express his sadness	Helped him deal with the death of his dog

everyone was reading them. The school librarian told him that there were sequels to *Locomotion* [*Peace, Locomotion* (Woodson, 2010)] and *Love That Dog* [*Hate That Cat* (Creech, 2010)]. She also gave him a stack of other novels in verse. He gave book talks on those books, too, and added them to the classroom library, where they were immediately checked out.

Poetry provided a real breakthrough for Jamal. Peter insisted on polished performances for Open Mike Fridays, and Jamal would practice reading and rereading poems aloud to meet the necessary standards for him to participate. The repeated readings helped to improve Jamal's fluency. Peter found the lyrics to popular rap songs for Jamal's poetry notebook. His familiarity with the songs helped to build his sight-word vocabulary. Jamal wasn't nearly as intimidated by poetry, with its short lines and all the white space on the page, as he was by text-dense prose. Jamal's reading log documented an increase in the number of books read, still mostly humorous poetry books and picture books. Jamal was more enthusiastic in reading conferences instead of monosyllabic and sullen. The conferences went on beyond the timer's buzz because Jamal wanted to read "just one more" poem to Peter. Providing a book closer to Jamal's reading level for this unit was not a miracle cure, but it did get Jamal to read more. Peter is hoping that the increase in the number of texts that Jamal is reading will lead to a real cure.

Now Peter could no longer use a single book for whole-class instruction in good conscience. His new challenge was to find a variety of books on the same topic to help better meet the collective instructional needs of all of his students.

WHOLE-CLASS INSTRUCTIONAL PRACTICE 5: USING DIFFERENTIATED TEXT SETS TO SUPPLEMENT CONTENT TEXTBOOKS

Fifth grader Tyreese had failed yet another social studies test. If something didn't change right away, he would definitely fail social studies for the entire quarter. Claudia, the interventionist, sighed as she read the note from Tyreese's classroom teacher informing her of the situation. Claudia got really annoyed when classroom teachers wanted her to help intervention students with their homework, book reports, science fair projects, or preparation for some test. She had her own goals for Tyreese— the goals that had been agreed upon in team meetings, based on assessment data. None of those goals had anything to do with social studies tests.

Claudia brought the note to the next literacy team meeting. She expected support from Debbie, the literacy coach, who instead said, "So, what are we going to do?"

Claudia was outraged! Why should she have to do anything at all? She was doing her assigned job. Tyreese was doing well in her intervention class. He had entered the program reading level

G texts during the third quarter of the last school year. Now he was reading level N texts because Claudia had consistently worked toward his goals. She hadn't abandoned the original goals each time a classroom teacher had been unhappy about something that the student had been doing in the regular classroom.

Debbie complimented Claudia on the wonderful work that she was doing with Tyreese. Seven text levels in a semester and a half is very impressive progress. But Debbie pointed out that Tyreese still needed to be able to function in the regular classroom. If there was something that Claudia could do to facilitate his success in the regular classroom, it would be worthy of her time and attention. Claudia sat fuming through the remainder of the meeting and stalked out of the room as soon as it was over.

Claudia had preliminary plans for Tyreese's group for the next two weeks. The group was reading *Tut, Tut* (Scieszka, 2004), a funny fantasy story about a group of boys who travel back in time and meet King Tut. The book was just at the border of Tyreese's instructional level, but he loved it and was willing to work hard to read it. The group had three other boys who loved the book as much as Tyreese. The boys had generated lots of questions about mummies and Ancient Egypt based on their reading. Claudia had had them record their questions in their journals and had brought in some informational books on the topic to help them find the answers. Tyreese had found a website on Ancient Egypt when he was in the computer lab. The boys had done some procedural writing on mummifying a corpse, had figured out how to write their names in hieroglyphics, and were currently investigating the curse of King Tut's tomb. It broke Claudia's heart to think about putting aside all of this engaged learning for some social studies textbook.

Claudia stopped in Tyreese's classroom at the end of the day to pick up a copy of the textbook and find out about the lesson goals for the upcoming weeks. She made it clear to Tyreese's teacher that she was not sure whether she could fit the social studies into her plans, but she was willing to investigate the possibility.

That evening, Claudia flipped through the pages of the unit. One of the things that immediately jumped out was how difficult the textbook seemed to be. She typed a couple of paragraphs into her word processing program to get a readability level. She was shocked and surprised to see that the Flesch-Kincaid level was 7.3. That couldn't be right! She carefully checked her typing. It was right. Her school was asking fifth graders to read a social studies textbook at a seventh-grade readability level. Even the students who were reading on level would have difficulty reading this book.

The next day, Claudia found Debbie and showed her what she had discovered. Debbie sampled a few more paragraphs from different parts of the textbook. The passages ranged in level from 6.1 to 7.8. Debbie told Claudia that Allington (2002) had written an article about this phenomenon about 10 years ago, so she wasn't particularly surprised. With the current emphasis on text complexity, it would be a hard sell to try to persuade the school to purchase easier textbooks. Besides, these textbooks were new! They were going to have to live with these books for at least the next four or five years. But without abandoning the current text-book, they needed to find a way to scaffold the students in a manner that would enable them to effectively learn the material despite the newly discovered difficulty. Since the textbook's readability level was two years above the grade in which it was actually being used, it was quite likely that Tyreese was not the only one having trouble with it. Debbie told Claudia that she would address the issue in the next fifth-grade team meeting. Claudia nodded and walked away smiling, relieved to have had that task taken off her to-do list.

Debbie's hunch was right. At the next fifth-grade team meeting, the teachers reported that a number of students were struggling with the new social studies textbook and failing tests. The teachers had attributed the difficulties to the students rather than to the textbook. The current class of fifth graders had more students who were "below grade level" and "approaching grade level" than the fifth-grade classes of previous school years.

Debbie offered to help the fifth-grade team plan the next social studies unit with the goal of making the information in the textbook accessible to all of their students. They gladly accepted her offer and scheduled another time to meet. Debbie asked the teachers to bring copies of the last social studies test that they had given, copies of some of their social studies lesson plans, and samples of student work.

At the next meeting, Debbie listened as the teachers talked about their artifacts. Their teaching seemed to rely heavily on the textbook and the supporting materials that had been provided with it. All of the samples of student work were worksheets from the textbook program. Their lesson plans were printouts provided by the textbook program, which included a teacher's edition, premade chapter and unit tests, worksheets, premade lesson plans, digital tools, and student study guides. The next unit in the social studies textbook was on the civil rights movement. The unit topics included

- school integration featuring Brown vs. the Board of Education,
- the Montgomery Bus Boycott,
- the Freedom Riders,
- the lunch counter sit-ins,
- the 1963 March on Washington, and
- the Civil Rights Act.

The unit had four chapters with a test at the end of each chapter and, finally, a unit test at the end of the unit. The teachers reported that they usually cover a chapter a week, or about a unit a month. They also reported that they do a presentation of each chapter's contents using the text-provided digital tools on their smartboards. Each chapter presentation takes place on a Monday. On Tuesday and Wednesday, the students are assigned to read the chapter, complete the worksheets, and complete the end-of-chapter questions. On Thursday, there is a chapter review, and the students receive a study guide. Finally, the test is given on Friday. This process is repeated the following week for the next chapter.

Debbie quickly decided that it would be a good idea to stick with the teachers' established schedule to help them feel more comfortable with her suggested changes. She encouraged them to continue with their Monday smartboard presentation for each chapter. However, instead of having the students tackle the textbook on Tuesday, she advocated putting them in small, mixed-ability groups to read some trade books on the chapter topic. Her proposal for Wednesday was for the groups to share what they had read in their trade books with the entire class, and then for the class to compare the information across books. After the book comparisons, she suggested, the small groups would reconvene to read the textbook.

The teachers frowned. Did it make sense to have the students read even more when some of them clearly weren't even reading the textbook? The teachers were skeptical that they would be able to succeed in getting the students to do the additional reading that would be expected of them using Debbie's plan. Debbie explained that the trade books—mostly picture books—would be a lot easier to read and probably more engaging, and they would also accomplish the important purpose of building the students' background knowledge and providing them with useful information on the topic. With background knowledge and some degree of familiarity with the topic, the students would be better prepared to take on the textbook. Also, they would be reading the textbook in mixed-ability groups rather than individually, which would enable them to support each other in reading the text.

Debbie looked at the teachers. They were still frowning. "What?" she asked. They wanted to know where they would get all of those trade books. Debbie assured them that she would help collect the books. She'd check the public libraries and the book rooms and the school libraries in the district. If she couldn't find what they needed there, she would see if there were any remaining funds available in the school's textbook budget.

The teachers slowly nodded. One of them asked, "Like literature circles?"

Debbie said, "Exactly, like literature circles! As a matter of a fact, you can structure Tuesday and Wednesday like a workshop. Do a minilesson and let the kids break up into small groups to read and talk. You won't have to do conferences, but you can still harness many of the advantages of small groups."

The teachers kept nodding. This was turning out better than Debbie had expected. She decided that this would be a good time to end the meeting.

Debbie sent out an email to the other literacy coaches in the district asking to borrow any available leveled books or trade books that they had in the book rooms or school libraries on the civil rights movement for fifth grade or lower. She also checked her own school library and book room as well as the public libraries in both the school community and her home district. Within a few days, she had amassed boxes of books. She put together the following text sets:

The Montgomery Bus Boycott

If a Bus Could Talk	Faith Ringgold
Rosa	Nikki Giovanni
The Bus Ride	William Miller
Freedom Walkers: The Story of the Montgomery Bus Boycott	Russell Freedman
Claudette Colvin: Twice Toward Justice	Phillip Hoose

School Integration

Remember: The Journey to School Integration	Toni Morrison
The Story of Ruby Bridges	Robert Coles
The School Is Not White	Doreen Rappaport
Remember Little Rock	Paul Robert Walker

Lunch Counter Sit-Ins

Freedom on the Menu: The Greensboro Sit-In	Carole Boston Weatherford
Sit In: How Four Friends Stood Up by Sitting Down	Andrea Pinkney

Freedom Riders

Freedom Riders: John Lewis and Jim Swerg on the Front Line of the Civil Rights Movement	Anne Bausum
Civil Rights Freedom Riders	Harriet Isecke
Freedom Rides: Journey for Justice	James Haskins

March on Washington

What Was the March on Washington?	Kathleen Krull
The March on Washington	L. S. Summer
We March	Shane W. Evans
The Sweet Smell of Roses	Angela Johnson
I Have a Dream	Kadir Nelson

The Civil Rights Act

The Civil Rights Act of 1964	Jason Skog
The Civil Rights Movement in America	Elaine Landau

Martin Luther King

Martin's Big Words	Doreen Rappaport
Who Was Martin Luther King?	Bonnie Bader
DK Biography: Martin Luther King, Jr.	Amy Pastan
A Picture Book of Martin Luther King	David Adler
If You Lived at the Time of Martin Luther King	Ellen Levine

Segregation in the South

White Socks Only	Evelyn Colman
A Taste of Colored Water	Matt Faulker
Freedom Summer	Deborah Wiles
Ruth and the Green Book	Calvin Alexander Ramsay
Goin' Someplace Special	Patricia McKissack
Richard Wright and the Library Card	Richard Wright

One of the literacy coaches brought Debbie a set of 10 leveled books published by Zaner-Bloser on the civil rights movement. There were six copies of each title. The books ranged from second- to sixth-grade readability levels. She also received several DVDs, including *Let Freedom Ring, Ruby Bridges,* and *Selma, Lord, Selma.* The textbook program's digital tools included a video of the "I Have a Dream" speech and some news footage of several of the marches.

Debbie delivered the boxes of books and materials to the fifth-grade classrooms and made sure to clear time in her schedule to drop in during social studies instruction. The students, who had experience with literature circles and book discussion, had no difficulty adjusting to the change. Debbie sat with a group of students who were reading a Martin Luther King biography. They read how King's philosophy of nonviolence was influenced by Gandhi. They asked her, "Who's Gandhi?" Debbie offered them an explanation, but she felt that it was inadequate, so she suggested that they also check online. The next time she was in that classroom, the group was reading Demi's picture book *Gandhi* (2001).

At the next fifth-grade team meeting, the teachers excitedly shared what was happening in their classrooms during social studies instruction. One teacher reported that one of her literature circles was reading *The Watsons Go to Birmingham—1963* (Curtis, 2001). The teachers remarked that they had learned a lot, too. For example, they had never previously heard of Claudette Colvin, so they hadn't had the slightest idea that someone was arrested for sitting in the white section of a bus before Rosa Parks.

The fifth-grade team looked ahead to the next unit on the Vietnam War. One of the teachers exclaimed, "We could use the book *The Wall* by Eve Bunting [1992]!" Another said, "Oh, and there's *The Lotus Seed* [Garland, 1997], too!" They were on their way.

Claudia sighed when Tyreese came into the intervention room a couple of weeks later with another envelope from his teacher. Inside the envelope was a copy of Tyreese's latest social studies test. Claudia looked it over and smiled. Tyreese got an 80.

A lot of learning took place in this story. Tyreese actually learned the contents of the social studies unit. After reading some picture and leveled books on the topic, he was better able to take on the social studies textbook with the support of his classmates. Tyreese learned how to look for and compare information across texts. Ideally, he'll be able to apply what he learned about the civil rights movement to future studies of history, government, civics, and life.

The fifth-grade teachers learned that it takes more than a textbook program to make content knowledge accessible to all of their students. The textbook is simply one tool. They have now filled the toolbox with many other tools, including

- a variety of texts at multiple levels and genres;
- digital tools; and
- established teaching practices such as literature discussion, text comparison charts, minilessons, and share time.

The experience reinforced what Debbie knew to begin with about professional learning: Teachers really do want their students to be successful. If you support them (plan with them, assemble materials for them, are present in the classroom for moral support), they will acquire the confidence to do it on their own.

Ideally, Claudia will learn that the true measure of success of an intervention program is what the student applies to reading and writing after leaving the intervention room, including the regular classroom setting and life outside of school as well.

Section Two

SMALL-GROUP AND INDIVIDUAL INSTRUCTIONAL PRACTICES

Finding meaningful, productive, and purposeful ways to engage struggling learners during whole-class instruction is essential. However, whole-class instruction is only half the story. The other half is implementing focused, targeted instruction that will aid in closing the achievement gap between the struggling learners and their on-level peers. If we do not focus on the goal of closing the gap, struggling students are destined to suffer from the "Monica syndrome"—making progress yet remaining below grade level.

The instructional practices described in this section take place in the regular classroom and are implemented by the regular classroom teacher, ideally in collaboration with any intervention specialists who might be working with the students (more on that later). This instruction is delivered in small groups and individually during the "work period" of literacy workshop.

The small groups are composed of students who have similar instructional needs. The instruction is designed to meet those specific needs. The teacher carefully plans these lessons, informed by formative assessment, using instructional-level texts to maximize the benefits for the students.

TRIED AND TRUE:
GUIDED READING

If you have students who are reading at a second-grade level or lower, one of the best things you can do for them is to engage them in regularly scheduled guided reading lessons. Tara turned up her nose at the idea. She taught fifth grade. The last thing she wanted to do was try to persuade 10-year-olds to sit at a kidney-shaped table and read leveled books. After all, these students were already going to intervention lessons three to four days a week. It was even Ivan's second year in intervention classes. During workshop time, they seemed to be happy enough reading easier books. Wasn't that sufficient? Tara's literacy coach, Claire, didn't think it was. She persuaded Tara to try guided reading with a group for just one month. Claire volunteered to plan with Tara and even model the first few lessons.

Every student in the school had taken a universal screening assessment, which confirmed that Brianna, Damarion, Quincy, and Ivan were definitely in need of special support. Claire told Tara that they would need more information to maximize the effectiveness of the proposed guided reading lessons. Claire got the data from the diagnostic assessments that were administered by the reading interventionist. From that data, Claire and Tara planned the first guided reading lesson.

Claire selected the book *Martin's Big Words* (Rappaport, 2001). She told Tara that even though the book was written at a second-grade level, it had rich content that would allow the group to discuss important concepts and ideas. The diagnostic data showed that Brianna, Damarion, Quincy, and Ivan were having difficulty reading multisyllabic words, struggling with even spoken vocabulary beyond the second-grade level, and showing little evidence of monitoring their reading. Claire and Tara would make sure to address all three of these issues in their plans.

Claire said that monitoring one's comprehension of text is critical. The simplest and most effective strategy for doing so is to stop and reread. *Martin's Big Words* is a good book for this strategy because each page is episodic, with three to five sentences, so it would be easy to go back and read any page again. Claire said that a short-term goal for the group was to get them in the habit of stopping and rereading whenever they realized that they didn't understand what was happening in the book.

Vocabulary and reading multisyllabic words would be addressed simultaneously. *Martin's Big Words* has numerous multisyllabic words. Claire recommended selecting a small number of content-specific words to focus the vocabulary/word study instruction. She and Tara picked *segregation, Southerners,* and *protested.*

Finally, they selected a "purpose for reading" the book that they wanted the students to keep in mind while reading it. They also prepared a (verbal) book introduction to convey the "purpose for reading" to the students. The central purpose of this particular book is to examine the words that Martin Luther King used to lead, inspire, and bring about change. Tara and Claire decided that the book's central purpose would be a good "purpose for reading." They would ask the students to identify the "big words" and decide what makes them "big."

Tara was surprised to discover that the guided reading lesson plan that she had written with Claire was very similar to the "close reading" lesson plans that she had written for the whole class. Close reading is careful, purposeful rereading of text (Fisher, Frey, & Lapp, 2012). That is exactly what was planned for this lesson. Each time the students would reread, it would be for a specific purpose. First, they would read to identify the "big words." Then they would read to monitor their comprehension. Finally, they would revisit the text yet another time to better understand content vocabulary. They would have to read the text three times—at least parts of it. Now Tara was particularly eager to see how this was going to work with the students who struggled most in the class.

Claire arrived the next day for the lesson. Tara was relieved that she was not dragging in a kidney-shaped table. Instead they all sat at a round table that her students used when they worked on group projects and had literature discussions. Claire distributed copies of the book, and the students immediately recognized it and began talking about it. Brianna reported that the librarian had read it aloud during Black History Month last year. Damarion said that Martin Luther King changed the laws so that black people could sit wherever they wanted to on the bus.

Quincy said, "Didn't he win the Pulitzer Prize?"

Claire smiled and said, "I am glad that you know so much about this book and Martin Luther King. What you already know will make it easier for you to understand what you are reading."

She gave the students index cards with the word *segregation* written on it. She asked them to draw lines to chunk the word into syllables. The students made reasonable divisions, were able to read the smaller chunks, and managed to put the chunks together to read the whole word. She had them do the same activity for *Southerners* and *protested*. Claire told them to look out for these words while they read the book and to use this strategy if they encountered any other words that they didn't know.

Then Claire introduced the book. She told the students that the book contained a collection of the "big words" that Martin Luther King used when he was doing important work to help the United States become a better country. She told them to see if they could identify the big words and the big idea behind each big word. Then she sent the students off to read.

Claire, followed by Tara, went around and listened to each of the students read, took a running record of their reading for one or two of the pages, and coached them to reread when they could not retell what had happened on a page and to use chunking when they encountered unfamiliar words. When the students had finished reading the book, Claire called them back to the table. She asked Tara to take notes during the discussion.

Claire asked, "What big word did you find, and what is the big idea behind your big word?"

Quincy said, "It wasn't the Pulitzer Prize. It was the Nobel Peace Prize. I think that *Nobel Peace Prize* is a big word and a big deal."

Claire said, "I agree with you. The Nobel Peace Prize is a big deal. You have learned something important. When you read, you can clear up some of the misunderstandings that you might have. *Nobel Peace Prize* is not one of *Martin's* big words. Can you find some big words that were Martin's?"

Brianna said, "I wrote down *dream*. But I think it is wrong."

"What makes you think it's wrong?" Claire asked.

"It's not that big," Brianna said.

"What about the big idea behind *dream*?" Claire asked.

"Well, that's a big deal," Brianna said. "It was a dream that the government would ever change laws. So many people didn't want the laws to change."

Claire said, "Go back into the book and find a passage that tells us that people didn't want the laws to change."

The students found multiple examples. They shared their other big words: *love, together,* and *courage.* Ivan said, "Two of our big words were little words."

Claire said, "Two of your words had only four or five letters, but the idea behind the words are very big."

After school, Claire and Tara got together to look at the notes from the day's lesson and to plan the next lesson. Claire showed Tara how to look at the running records to understand the students' reading behaviors and to use that information to plan the next lessons. She told her to look at the notes from the students' discussion to think about their comprehension. Claire told Tara that guided reading is both the teacher guiding the students while they are reading and the students' reading behaviors guiding the teacher in planning lessons to help them improve. Tara told Claire how similar this guided reading lesson was to her "close reading" lessons. Claire said, "I think 'close reading' is just another form of guided reading, especially when we first introduce it to students. Eventually, students will do it on their own."

Claire taught the guided reading lessons for the first week while Tara watched. Tara and Claire taught together during the second week. Tara taught the lessons for the third week while Claire watched and coached her. Tara taught the lessons alone during the last week, but Claire met with her to review the running records and the anecdotal notes. They carefully selected books for future lessons that were at the students' instructional level and would help them work toward their goals of monitoring comprehension, enhancing vocabulary, and word solving multisyllabic words. They also wanted books that were engaging and appealing.

Claire administered the Developmental Reading Assessment after the trial month. Tara was surprised and delighted to learn that three of the students had progressed one level. Damarion improved but fell slightly below the cutoff for the next level. The experience made a believer out of Tara.

TRIED AND TRUE: A GUIDED READING RESOURCE LIST

Claire immediately reached for picture books to teach Brianna, Quincy, and Damarion. Picture books are often overlooked as a resource when planning small-group reading instruction for students beyond the primary grades. Teachers assume that students in the third to sixth grades will be resistant to working in a group reading picture books. The reality is that picture books play a very important role in instruction for the middle and upper grades. Teachers routinely use picture books in minilessons and for mentor texts. If a teacher is concerned about possible "picture book rejection," one seemingly paradoxical solution could be to increase the use of picture books. You can pair novels with picture books on the same topic or by the same author. You can use picture books to complement math, content, and fine arts instruction. You can read picture books aloud to your third, fourth, fifth, and sixth graders.

Here is a starter list of great picture books to use for guided reading with struggling learners in grades three through six:

Say, Allen (2008). *Grandfather's Journey*. Houghton Mifflin. The narrator tells the story of his grandfather's immigration to America pieced together through photographs in a picture album and remembered family stories. Issues addressed include acculturation and assimilation.

Pair this book with *Dragonwings* (Yep, 2001) or *A Jar of Dreams* (Uchida, 1993).

Gerstein, Mordicai (2007). *The Man Who Walked Between the Towers*. Square Fish. In 1974, Philip Petit somehow managed to sneak up onto the roofs of the Twin Towers, attach a tightrope, and walk across. The people of New York City were mesmerized. A good book for remembering happier times on September 11.

Pair this book with *I Survived the Attacks of September 11, 2001* (Tarshis, 2012) or *Betti on the High Wire* (Railsback, 2010).

Burleigh, Robert (2001). *Hoops*. HMH Books for Young Readers. The fabulous illustrations and sparse poetic text capture the movement, feel, and passion of urban kids playing basketball on a hot summer day.

Pair this book with *The Moves Make the Man* (Brooks, 1994) or *Taking Sides* (Soto, 2003).

Winter, Jeannette (2005). *The Librarian of Basra: A True Story from Iraq*. HMH Books for Young Readers. As war looms, Alia Muhammad Baker takes action to save the books in the public library. A good book for discussing the unintended consequences of war. A more poignant book on this theme is *The Faithful Elephants* (Tsuchiya, 1997).

Pair this book with *Dear Blue Sky* (Sullivan, 2012) or even *The Hunger Games* (Collins, 2008).

Mochizuki, Ken (1995). *Baseball Saved Us*. Lee and Low. The Japanese keep their spirits up in the internment camps by playing baseball. Good book to use during a unit on World War II.

Pair this book with *Weedflower* (Kadohata, 2008) or *Dear Miss Breed* (Oppenheimer, 2006).

Yim Bridges, Shirin (2002). *Ruby's Wish*. Chronicle Books.
Unlike most girls in turn-of-the-century China, Ruby does not want to grow up and get married. She wants to go to the university.
Pair this book with *Chu Ju's House* (Whelan, 2008).

Piven, Hanoch (2012). *What Presidents Are Made Of*. Atheneum
Books.
A cleverly illustrated book on well-known and obscure facts about the presidents of the United States. Another great book about the presidents is *So, You Want to Be President* (St. George, 2004). A great way to celebrate Presidents' Day.
Good novels to pair with these books include *Bully for You, Teddy Roosevelt* (Fritz, 1997) and *Lincoln: A Photobiography* (Freedman, 1989).

Bunting, Eve (1999). *Smoky Nights*. HMH Books for Young Readers.
Neighbors become unlikely allies as they huddle together in a safer place during riots in Los Angeles.
Pair this Caldecott winner with *One Crazy Summer* (Williams-Garcia, 2010).

Van Allsburg, Chris (1991). The Wretched Stone. Houghton
Mifflin.
A crew of sailors brings a strange, glowing stone onto their ship. Gradually, they abandon all their duties and spend the day staring at the stone. Almost all of Chris Van Allsburg's books will work for guided reading with older students.
Some people think that the wretched stone is actually television, so pull it out when the character Mike Teevee is introduced in *Charlie and the Chocolate Factory* (Dahl, 2007).

Gaiman, Neil (2005). *Wolves in the Walls*. HarperCollins.
Lucy is convinced that there are wolves in the walls of her house. Her parents and brother tell her not to be silly, that it's probably just mice. But Lucy is right.
Neil Gaiman is a prolific author. Pair this book with any of his novels such as *Coraline* (2009), *The Graveyard Book* (2009), or *The Sandman* (2011).

Smith, Lane (2006). *John, Paul, George, and Ben.* Hyperion.
An entertaining look at the founding fathers and how their
personal traits—good and bad—were instrumental in the
founding of our country.

Pair this book with *Chains* (Halse, 2011), *The Fighting
Ground* (Avi, 2009), or *Johnny Tremain* (Forbes, 1998).

Shine, Andrea (1999). *The Summer My Father Was Ten.* Boyds
     Mills Press.
Every year while working in the garden, a little girl's father tells
her the story of the summer he was 10. The father and his
friends vandalize a neighbor's garden. Sure to be a catalyst for a
discussion on vandalism.

Pair this book with *Hoot* (Hiassen, 2005).

Woodson, Jacqueline (2012). *Each Kindness.* Nancy Paulsen
     Books.
A new girl enrolls in school and becomes the subject of
ridicule. This book generates insightful discussions and writing.

Pair this book with *The Hundred Dresses* (Estes, 2004).

Golenbock, Peter (1992). *Teammates.* HMH Books for Young
     People.
The story of the friendship between Jackie Robinson and Pee
Wee Reese.

Pair this book with *In the Year of the Boar and Jackie Robinson*
(Lord, 2003).

CONFERRING WITH READERS TO FIND THE RIGHT SERIES

A goal for all struggling learners is to increase the amount of reading they do. Anything that we want to learn to do better—shooting baskets, playing the piano, the breaststroke, or the cha-cha—improves when we practice, practice, practice. As an observant student once said, "If they don't read much, how they ever gonna get good?" (Allington, 1977). One of the best tools available for achieving the goal of reading more is to engage students in reading series books. If you can find a series that a struggling learner likes and wants to read, you will be well on your way to achieving the goal of increasing the volume of reading.

Series books are perfect for struggling learners. They have been credited with leading to significant improvement in the reading progress of struggling learners (Richek & McTeague, 1988). Scaffolding is built right into the books. Once a reader has met the characters and become familiar with their personalities as well as the settings and predictable situations in the story, the book becomes easier to read. The familiarity and predictability is encouraging and supportive to struggling learners, spurring them on to the next book in the series.

If you can find a series connected with one of the readers' interests, such as Angel Park Soccer Stars (Hughes) for soccer fans, Pony Pals (Betancourt) for "horse-crazy" girls, or Legos City Adventures (Sanders) for the "Lego maniacs," all the better. Their background knowledge on the topic provides yet another scaffold! With more than 3,500 series currently available for kids, there is sure to be one for every reader. Your job is to find it.

Jaden is a friendly, outgoing fourth grader. He always has a smile on his face and is surrounded by lots of friends. He really likes coming to school. He is good at math, and the classroom pet, a guinea pig named Clarence, really likes him. Whenever he approaches the cage, Clarence squeaks until Jaden takes him out and scratches his head. At recess, Jaden is always in the center of a group of boys who enjoy playing with Lego mini-figures, matchbox cars, and action figures. These boys are always planning elaborate adventures for their toys. Before the implementation of the strategy described immediately below, Jaden thought that school was just perfect, except for one thing—he didn't like reading at all.

Jaden's teacher, Dana, was becoming increasingly aware of his difficulties with reading. With the increased use of content textbooks in the fourth grade, Jaden's problems were becoming more pronounced. He was certainly bright enough, and Dana was sure that his reading would get better if he would only practice. Jaden didn't fully take advantage of independent-reading time. As a matter of fact, Dana strongly suspected that he was engaged in "fake reading" (Tovani, 2000). Several clues evoked this suspicion:

(a) Whenever Dana scanned the room during independent-reading time, Jaden looked just like the other students. He had a book in his hands and seemed to be reading it. However, when she stole a quick glance at him, she'd see his eyes immediately dart back to the page.

(b) Jaden's reading log listed multiple abandoned books. His reason for abandoning a book was usually that it was "boring."

(c) During reading conferences, Jaden made only vague comments about the books listed as "completed" on his reading log. When Dana tried to engage him in a real conversation about a book, Jaden would attempt to distract her with questions about her dog, her running—

anything but the book. He was also a master of the "text-to-self tangent."

With the pressure to get in more conferences, Dana had allowed him to get away with his ploys thus far. Now she was determined to find out if her suspicions were on target. At the next conference, she asked Jaden to take out the book he was currently reading. After some rummaging around in his independent-reading baggie, he finally pulled out a battered copy of *Freckle Juice* (Blume, 1978).

Dana said, "Don't you feel sorry for Andrew? He's the only one in his family who has freckles." Jaden launched into one of his text-to-self tangents about being the only one in his family with curly hair.

Dana stopped him midsentence. She said, "I know that you have not read *any* of this book." She opened the book to the first page, handed it to Jaden, and asked him to read it aloud.

He laboriously read, "Andrew Marcus always wanted freckles." Jaden's smile faded, and he looked down at his shoes. Dana gently told him that she'd really like to help him find some books that he would enjoy reading. She sent Jaden back to his work area to complete an interest inventory.

Armed with the information from the interest inventory, Jaden's independent-reading level, and what Dana knew about him, she found the perfect series for him—the Fluffy the Guinea Pig series (McMullan). These books are written at a second-grade level, so Jaden would be able to read with them with ease. Fluffy was a classroom pet, just like Clarence, their classroom guinea pig. The stories were told from Fluffy's perspective. Given Jaden's sense of humor, Dana thought that he'd find the books funny.

Dana won Jaden over by reading aloud the passage in *Fluffy Goes to School* (McMullan, 1999), in which Fluffy learns that the class has decided to name him Fluffy, which he doesn't like at all. Dana and Jaden did a shared reading of the next couple of pages. Finally, Jaden read aloud a page or two on his own while Dana listened. Then Dana sent him off to finish the book independently.

Jaden actually finished reading the book and had a very animated conversation with Dana about it. He had really enjoyed reading about the smart-aleck, wise-cracking guinea pig. Jaden wondered what Clarence was thinking and what his squeaks meant. Dana was excited about his response. There are more than a dozen Fluffy books. That would be enough to keep Jaden reading for several weeks, giving Dana sufficient time to find the next series. She offered Jaden another Fluffy book, *Fluffy Goes Apple Picking* (McMullan, 2002).

Unfortunately, the next book didn't go over nearly as well. Jaden abandoned it after only a few pages of the 40-page book. He couldn't believe that any teacher would ever agree to take a guinea pig on a field trip. Dana could see his point. Jaden thought the book would have been a lot funnier and more believable if Wade had smuggled Fluffy out of the classroom and taken him on the trip. Then, of course, Fluffy would get lost in the orchard and Wade would have to confess to taking Fluffy on the trip. Dana complimented him on his critical response and encouraged him to write his own version of the story.

However, it became apparent that the all-too-brief love affair with Fluffy was over. When Dana tried to get him to read *Fluffy's School Bus Adventure* (McMullan, 2001), Jaden started to complain. He said the Fluffy books were "kindergarten books." So she sent him off to the classroom library to find a book on his own—a book that she knew he wouldn't read. Dana had to go back to the drawing board.

Where had Dana gone wrong? Fluffy is a series book from the "Hello Reader" collection, books written for children who have recently learned how to read. Although the series was at Jaden's reading level, it was below his interest level. One of the books in the series amused him. However, the series as a whole did not maintain his interest. That is one of the big challenges of finding books for struggling readers. The books that they are able to read are usually below their interest level.

Dana pitched several series to Jaden in the next couple of weeks, including Horrible Harry (Kline), My Weird School (Gutman), and the A to Z Mysteries (Roy). The results were always the same. Jaden would take the book and abandon it within a day or two. It was getting really discouraging, but Dana was determined not to give up.

She talked to her colleagues and librarians. She searched the Internet and browsed bookstores. She made lists and listened to recommendations. Finally, she had collected a set of several series that she thought might work. She decided to start by trying *Ricky Ricotta's Mighty Robot* (Pilkey, 2000), the first book in a series written at the second- and third-grade reading levels. The main character in the series has his own giant robot. Jaden loves action figures and imaginative play. It had an excellent chance of working.

Instead of offering the book directly to Jaden, Dana did a book talk on series books for the entire class. The students were asked to sign up if they were interested in starting one of the series. The book talk generated a lot of enthusiasm, and the students were clamoring to write their names on the sign-up sheets. Unfortunately, Jaden didn't bite. However, several of Jaden's friends signed up to start the Ricky Ricotta series.

Dana asked the boys if they wanted to form a Ricky Ricotta book club. They enthusiastically agreed. She gave each member of the group a small sketchpad to try their hand at drawing the characters according to the instructions provided in the book. The first Ricky Ricotta book club meeting was so boisterous that Dana had them convene in the hall, right outside the classroom door. When Dana stole glances at Jaden during workshop, she saw him longingly watching his friends having fun talking about Ricky Ricotta.

After recess, Jaden approached her and asked to be included in the Ricky Ricotta book club. Dana replied that the group had already been formed and had completed part of the book. She told Jaden that joining would mean catching up—reading everything he had missed so far and also being ready to discuss the current chapter at the next meeting. Jaden said he would do it. Dana handed him a copy of the book and wished him luck.

Throughout the day, Dana saw Jaden stealing time to read during transitions. At the end of the day, she saw him put the book in his backpack. The following morning, Jaden absolutely exploded into the classroom waving his copy of *Ricky Ricotta's Mighty Robot*. "I read the whole thing, Mrs. Alton! All hundred and twenty-eight pages! I started reading and I couldn't stop!"

She replied, "Great! Remember, you can't talk about anything beyond the designated chapter in your book club meeting today."

When it was time for workshop, Jaden took his book and joined the Ricky Ricotta book club in the hall right outside the classroom door. After a few minutes, he came back in and asked for his own sketchpad.

Dana had done it! She had found the right series for Jaden. She already had copies of *Ricky Ricotta's Giant Robot vs. The Mutant Mosquitos from Mercury* (Pilkey, 2000) and the next few books in the series ready for when the group would need them.

Jaden did not become a voracious reader overnight, but he slowly and steadily increased the amount that he read. His reading log had more and more completed books. The abandoned books were few and far between. Dana kept Jaden on her radar and tried to keep some books stashed away that he might enjoy. After the Ricky Ricotta series, Jaden read the Bionicle series (Farshtey) and the Commander Toad series (Yolen). Eventually, he even read a nonseries book, *Fourth Grade Rats* (Spinelli, 1993), which was a bit of stretch for him.

Dana convened a short-term small group, which included Jaden, to work on strategies for selecting books for independent reading. She was pleased that she had experienced some success in getting Jaden to read more, but she also wanted him to be self-reliant. If he was ever going to lead a "readerly life," he could not sit around waiting for Dana to pick his next book—he had to learn to do it for himself.

The other members of the group completed interest inventories, like Jaden had done a couple of months earlier. They identified the qualities in books that they had enjoyed reading in the past. They identified people who had made recommendations that had worked out for them. Dana supported the group in making more meaningful entries in their reading logs, so that the logs could serve as a resource in the future. Finally, Dana showed them some online resources that could support them in selecting books.

In review, here are the recommended steps for increasing students' volume of reading by means of matching them to appropriate series of books. (1) Have the students complete an interest inventory (see the interest inventory on page 71). (2) Find series at both the students' reading levels and their interest levels. Dana's first attempt with Jaden was only briefly successful because the series failed to maintain his interest over the long term. (3) Support the students in reading the first book, using gradual release. At least in the first attempt, Dana read aloud the first pages, engaged Jaden in a shared reading for the next few pages, and listened to him read the next pages. Then she sent Jaden off to read on his own. In Jaden's case, gradual release turned out to be unnecessary with the series that had the greatest success, but this is the exception rather than the rule.

Dana continued supporting Jaden by touching base with him more frequently, getting him involved in a book club, monitoring his reading log, and looking out for books that he might like. Finally, she explicitly taught him strategies for finding and selecting books on his own.

Here is a starter list of series books arranged by reading levels. You are encouraged to make the list even more useful by making omissions or adding series that are published later than this book.

First Grade

The number of series books for students who are reading at first-grade reading levels is limited. There are virtually no series books available for students reading at the earliest first-grade levels (guided reading levels C–F), except for leveled books that happen to be part of a series, such as Mrs. Wishy Washy, Greedy Cat, Bella and Rosie, *and* The Meanies.

Elephant and Piggie	Mo Willems
Fly Guy	Tedd Arnold
Little Bear	Else Holmelund Minarik

Second Grade

Fluffy	Kate McMullan
Amelia Bedelia	Peggy Parish
The Magic Treehouse	Mary Pope Osborne

Little Bill	Bill Cosby
Henry and Mudge	Cynthia Rylant
Poppleton	Cynthia Rylant
Mr. Putter and Tabby	Cynthia Rylant
Frog and Toad	Arnold Lobel
Adventures of Benny and Watch	Gertrude Warner
Ricky Ricotta's Mighty Robot	Dav Pilkey
Junie B. Jones	Barbara Park
Cam Jansen	David Adler
Nate the Great	Marjorie Weinman Sharmot
Stink	Megan McDonald
My Weird School	Dan Gutman
Bailey School Kids	Debbie Dadey
The Kids From Polk Street School	Patricia Reilly Giff

Third Grade

Captain Underpants	Dav Pilkey
The Zack Files	Dan Greenburg
Bionicle	Greg Farshtey
The Boxcar Children	Gertrude Warner
Chet Gecko	Bruce Hale
Judy Moody	Megan McDonald
Wayside School	Louis Sachar
A to Z Mysteries	Ron Roy
Horrible Harry	Suzy Kline
The Magic School Bus chapter books	Eva Moore, et al.
Arthur chapter books	Marc Brown
Vet Volunteers	Laurie Hasse Anderson
Clementine	Sara Pennypacker

Fourth Grade

The Spiderwick Chronicles	Tony DiTerlizzi
The Time Warp Trio	Jon Scieszka
Animorphs	K. A. Applegate
39 Clues	Rick Riordan, et al.
Alex Ryder	Anthony Horowitz
My Name Is America	Jim Murphy, et al.
The American Girls	Valerie Tripp, et al.

Percy Jackson	Rick Riordan
Wendy the Horse Gentler	Dandi Daley Mackall
Moxie Maxwell	Peggy Gifford
The Cheetah Girls	Deborah Gregory
Sammy Keyes	Wendelin Van Draanen
Big Nate	Lincoln Peirce
Wimpy Kid	Jeff Kinney

Here is a sample of an interest inventory that you can use to help you find out more about the readers in your class.

Interest Inventory Survey

Name _____

1. The best book I've ever read is _____
   _____

2. My favorite TV show is _____
   _____

3. The best movie I've ever seen is _____
   _____

4. My favorite game is _____
   _____

5. At recess, I like to _____
   _____

6. If someone wanted to give me a great present, it would be _____
   _____

7. If I got to plan a field trip for our class, I would go to _____
   _____

8. The next time there is no school, I wish I could _____
   _____

WORD STUDY—A LITTLE
GOES A LONG WAY

Let's address the elephant in the room. Word study is the favored, go-to instructional strategy for all struggling learners. Teachers run to it so often that most struggling learners have been thoroughly steeped in phonics by the time they reach third grade. These students have completed reams of phonics worksheets and piles of phonics workbooks. When struggling learners finally get the opportunity to practice applying the phonics lessons to actual reading, it is likely to be with the stilted, artificial language of a decodable book. Phonics skill practice—rather than actually reading and discussing interesting books, practicing strategies, and writing—has dominated their small-group lessons. In spite of all those phonics lessons, these students are still reading below grade-level expectations.

Teachers are likely to retort that their struggling learners really need phonics lessons. These students have difficulty solving words when they are reading, and their writing contains spelling errors that show an apparent lack of knowledge about vowels and consonant clusters.

So what's a teacher to do? Sandra asked herself that question as she examined the beginning-of-the-year screening assessment results for her third-grade class. The data revealed that three of her students, Kylie, Colin, and Blake, were definite outliers. They scored significantly below the rest of the class. After three years of literacy instruction, they were still reading at the first-grade level. The beginning-of-the-year universal screening assessment and samples of their in-class writing made Sandra suspect that they probably needed additional support in phonics. To her credit, she did not immediately launch these students into yet another intensive word study program. She decided to administer an additional assessment to verify her suspicions and to determine the students' specific needs for word study.

Sandra administered the Primary Spelling Inventory (Bear, et al., 2011) to the entire class. The additional information about the other students would be informative in planning whole-class minilessons. The spelling inventory was quick and easy to administer, like a spelling test. Kylie, Colin, and Blake misspelled more than half of the 26 words on the assessment. An analysis of their errors indicated that as a group, they struggled with

- confusion with long-vowel patterns CVCe (consonant-vowel-consonant followed by silent *e*) and CVVC (consonant-vowel-vowel-consonant),
- long-vowel pattern *–igh*,
- *r*-controlled vowel patterns,
- beginning and ending consonant clusters, and
- vowel diphthongs.

The analysis also showed that the students' strengths in word solving included

- regular CVC patterns,
- initial diagraphs, and
- beginning and ending consonants.

Knowing their competencies in word solving would also assist Sandra in planning instruction for them.

She looked more closely at the students' writing samples and running records. This examination revealed that the miscues in their reading and the misspellings in their writing were consistent with the results of the spelling inventory.

Armed with this important information, Sandra was ready to start small-group instruction for Kylie, Colin, and Blake. She decided to make working with this group every day for 20 to 30 minutes a priority. That meant that the other groups would meet with her two to three days a week. Although it was tempting to focus the instruction for Kylie, Colin, and Blake on their word-solving deficits, Sandra knew that isolated word study would be a dead end. It hadn't yielded sufficiently positive results thus far. In addition to acquiring grade-level word-solving skills, these three students needed to be able to apply what they had learned in a word study lesson to actual reading and writing. So Sandra had to give them many opportunities to read and write.

Sandra selected *Willie's Wonderful Pet* (Cebulash, 1993) for the first lesson. She thought that the book was a good choice for a number of reasons. First of all, it was the size and shape of the books that other students in the class were reading, such as *Skinnybones* (Park, 1997), *The Mouse and the Motorcycle* (Cleary, 1990), and *Judy Moody* (MacDonald, 2010). Yes, it was a skinny book. It had many fewer pages than the books that the other students were reading, but it wasn't one of those "written-for-instructional-purposes leveled books" that shouted "slow reader" to the whole world. She acknowledged that *Willie's Wonderful Pet* isn't great literature. However, it is about something. It tells a real story about a boy who doesn't have a pet to bring to school for Pet Day but comes up with an ingenious solution. Finally, this book would help Sandra meet her instructional word study goals without sounding awkward and stilted like books that are overtly phonetically regular. The book has many regular CVC words (*cat, get, pet, can, his, cup, . . .*) to boost the students' confidence in reading. It also has words with the spelling patterns that Kylie, Colin, and Blake needed to practice: *r*-controlled vowels, vowel diphthongs, and long-vowel patterns.

Sandra decided to focus her first word study lessons on the long-*a* spelling patterns -*ay* and CaCe. She did a brief minilesson on these spelling patterns and had the three students read and write the words *day, way, may, stay, came, late, gave,* and *vase* on their dry erase boards. Sandra quickly constructed a word pattern chart for -*ay* and CaCe. Then the students did a word sort. She checked the timer. The word study part of the lesson took six minutes, about a fourth of the time she had allotted for this lesson. She'd have to tighten this up in future lessons. Once the routines became established, she was sure that it would go a lot faster.

Then Sandra did an introduction for *Willie's Wonderful Pet* and engaged the students in a guided reading of the book. As Sandra listened in on the students' reading, she was gratified to see that the word study lesson seemed to be paying off. Both Kylie and Blake read *day* and *play* accurately. However, the CaCe words in the text were still "a work in progress." Blake read *same* as *small*, and Colin read *came* as *come*. She was able to coach Blake through an accurate reading of *same* by referring him to the word pattern chart and having him write the word on the dry erase board. Of course, she directed him to reread the entire page (keeping in mind that there were only two sentences on the page). However, the teacher-student coaching ended up making Colin agitated, so Sandra just told him the word. Well, it was only the first lesson. She did not expect miracles, but she was encouraged with her first efforts.

After the reading, they discussed the story and briefly reviewed the -*ay* and CaCe patterns. Then Sandra sent the students back to independent work time in workshop. They took the word sort in an envelope, a copy of the book for their independent-reading baggies, and a written-response assignment. She encouraged Kylie, Colin, and Blake to reread the book and practice the sort. Sandra made a neater copy of the word pattern chart for future reference. She planned to revisit *Willie's Wonderful Pet* as a touchstone text when she taught *r*-controlled vowels and vowel diphthongs.

Sandra's small-group lesson structure to help students increase proficiency in word solving includes the following components:

- word study minilesson
- word study activity
- guided reading
- discussion
- word study review
- written response

Each 20–30-minute lesson begins with a brief, explicit mini-lesson on a specific word study element, followed by a hands-on word study activity for practice. The hands-on activity can include word sorts, making words, word ladders, or word writing on individual whiteboards. Sandra and her students made small-group-size anchor charts (as opposed to whole-class-size) for each element that they studied. Sandra retired each anchor chart as the students became proficient with the applicable word study element. She made standard-size copies (8½ by 11 inches) of the anchor charts to glue into Kylie's, Colin's, and Blake's reading notebooks. After the word study activity, the small-group lesson structure concludes with a guided reading lesson, followed by a quick review of the word study minilesson and a written response.

When the students had a particularly difficult time learning a word study element, Sandra engaged them in a shared writing of a short story with multiple uses of the word study element instead of a guided reading lesson.

Sandra readministered the Primary Spelling Inventory every five weeks to assess their progress and make sure that her lessons were on target.

USING POETRY
AS A FOCUS TEXT

One of the best genres for teaching struggling learners is poetry. Poetry is user-friendly and not at all intimidating. When a struggling learner approaches a poem, she sees a page with plenty of white space. She is immediately put at ease. You can almost hear her sigh in relief. Instead of pushing the text away, she is more likely to attempt to read it.

Poetry comes with its own built-in scaffolds. The rhyme and rhythm support a reader's expectations of upcoming words. Poems often have repeated words. Once a reader has decoded a word, she often has multiple opportunities to read it again. By the end of the poem, that word just might have become part of her sight-word vocabulary. Poetry helps to build a reader's confidence and increases the probability that she will be willing to take on some prose.

Poetry can be used to teach word analysis, fluency, comprehension, and vocabulary. The brevity of the genre allows a teacher to squeeze in a powerful lesson when there is not a lot of time available. By selecting the right poem, you can engage the most unmotivated reader.

Sandra discovered that poetry was a valuable resource in working with Kylie, Colin, and Blake. She accidentally backed into using poetry. During one of their small-group lessons, a commotion arose in the hall outside their classroom door. Sandra quipped, "Three, four, shut the door." Kylie thought the comment was funny and dissolved into giggles. The giggles were contagious, and soon Colin and Blake joined in.

Sandra said, "That's part of an old children's rhyme. Don't you know it?" They didn't. So she quickly jotted down the rhyme on the group-size whiteboard:

One, two, buckle my shoe
Three, four, shut the door
Five, six, pick up sticks
Seven, eight, lay them straight
Nine, ten, a big fat hen

They were able to read the rhyme with little difficulty (except that Sandra had to support them in figuring out *straight*) on the first attempt, which delighted them.

Sandra had planned to address *r*-controlled /o/ in the word study component of the lesson that day. She underlined the line "Three, four, shut the door" and asked the students to identify the rhyming words. They quickly responded with *four* and *door*. Sandra talked briefly about *r*-controlled vowels and how when a word has an *r*-controlled /o/, it can be spelled -*or*, -*ore*, or -*our*. She created a word pattern chart for the /o/ *r*-controlled spelling patterns. They continued the lesson, reading the book *Morris the Moose* (Wiseman, 1991). The students were successful in reading the *r*-controlled /o/ words in that book.

Sandra was surprised by how much that little rhyme had delighted Kylie, Colin, and Blake. She had to admit to herself that the small-group lessons had become a little humdrum lately. There was no spark of delight in their eyes when the students read about Morris the Moose, the Fire Cat, or Sammy the Seal. Maybe a poetry break was exactly what they needed.

For the next day's lesson, Sandra selected a classic children's poem, "Eletelephony," by Laura Richards, because it's short and silly and offers an opportunity to do some focused word study. She reasoned that since Kylie, Colin, and Blake had so thoroughly enjoyed "One, Two, Buckle My Shoe," they would not be able to resist "Eletelephony."

She wrote the poem on an 11-by-17-inch sheet of cardstock. Then she prepared standard-size copies (8½ by 11 inches) of "Eletelephony" and "One, Two, Buckle My Shoe" and put them in folders. She started the lesson by inviting the students to read the poem silently first, and then she led them in a shared reading of the poem on the enlarged copy.

Eletelephony
by Laura Richards
Once there was an elephant,
Who tried to use the telephant-
No! No! I mean an elephone
Who tried to use the telephone-
(Dear me! I am not certain quite
That even now I've got it right.)

However it was, he got his trunk
Entangled in the telephunk;
The more he tried to get it free,
The louder buzzed the telephee-
(I fear I'd better drop the song
Of elephop and telephong!)

As Sandra expected, the students stumbled through the nonsense words: *telephant, elephone, telephunk, telephee, elephop,* and *telephong.* This opened the door to a minilesson on the chunking strategy for problem solving unknown words. Blake even remarked that you couldn't use "What makes sense?" or "Does it look right?" to help figure out the words in this situation. Sandra reinforced the idea that readers needed to be ready with a variety of problem-solving strategies. Within minutes, the students were reading the poem fluently between giggles.

Colin said, "I wonder what it looked like with the telephone cord tangled around its trunk."

"I wonder, too," Sandra said. "Why don't you draw a picture to show what you think it might have looked like?" She gave each of the students a blank piece of paper for their drawings and their new poetry notebooks, and she asked them to bring the notebooks along whenever their group got together.

Sandra designated Wednesday as Poetry Day. Each Wednesday, she introduces a new poem, and the group does a shared reading of it. Although most poems offer a variety of teaching opportunities, Sandra teaches just a single focus lesson based on the poem. The lesson might be a

- word study lesson based on a phonics element used in the poem;
- word study lesson based on a word structure element, such as prefixes, suffixes, inflectional endings, or compound words;
- vocabulary lesson; or
- comprehension lesson.

After the focus lesson, the group rereads the poem. At the students' insistence, each student selects a past poem to read aloud to the group. For the writing component of the lesson, the group does a written response that is often an imitation of (or an innovation based on) the new poem.

On the other days that the group meets, they proceed with their regular lesson structure, now with an added fluency component—the choral reading of the poem of the week. The modified structure is as follows:

- choral reading of the poem of the week
- word study minilesson
- word study activity
- guided reading
- discussion
- word study review
- written response

Despite the component that has been added to the small-group lesson framework, the lesson is still only 20 to 30 minutes long. A choral reading of a poem adds about a minute to the lesson. However, that minute helps to improve the students' fluency, increase their sight-word vocabularies, and bring joy to their small-group lesson.

MINILESSON
FOLLOW-UP SESSION

By the time a struggling learner has reached third grade, he has often become proficient in the use of a well-developed set of "school survival" strategies. These strategies are designed to help him fit in, save face, and avoid humiliating situations such as having to read aloud or not having the correct answer to the teacher's question. One of these strategies is "flying under the radar." He will try to be as inconspicuous as possible. He'll attempt to blend into the background and carefully avoid any eye contact with the teacher.

During a minilesson, the struggling learner is likely to be the very last one to arrive at the whole-group meeting area. Maybe she'll sit on the outer boundaries of the group, keeping her head down, flipping through her book or response journal. Maybe she'll have to stop and tie her shoelaces. These avoidance strategies take a bit of concentration. It is no wonder the struggling learner often misses some, or even big chunks, of the instruction presented in minilessons.

Sometimes it might therefore be necessary to schedule a small-group follow-up session. Fifth-grade teacher Rhonda found it necessary to follow up on her "point of view" minilesson using the book *Seedfolks* (Fleischman, 2004) as a mentor text. She had selected *Seedfolks* because it was a familiar book for her class. She had previously read chapters of the book in a shared-reading lesson, and many of her students had read the entire book for independent reading.

The minilesson contrasted a first-person and third-person telling of a story and how it affects the story. Rhonda and her students discussed the following questions: Who is telling the story? How do we know what the character is thinking and feeling? How does the point of view affect the story? Students were instructed to consider their current independent-reading book. Rhonda provided the following prompt for her students to respond to in their reader response journals:

What point of view is your book written in? How does the point of view affect the story?

During sharing time, some of the students shared the perspective of the books that they were reading and how it affected their understanding of the story. Antonio was reading *The Diary of a Wimpy Kid* (Kinney, 2007). He correctly identified it as being written in the first person. He said that he knew exactly what Greg (the main character) was thinking and feeling because the book is a diary. A diary is a place to write about your thoughts and feelings. Stefanie was reading *Little House in the Big Woods* (Ingalls Wilder, 2004). She reported that it is written in the third person. Stefanie could infer what Laura was thinking and feeling, but it did not explicitly say this in the book.

Rhonda was feeling pretty good about the lesson after share time. Then she started responding to the reader response journals. It became clear to her that some of the struggling learners in her class did not completely understand point of view. For example, this was Anita's reader response journal entry:

Changes for Molly [Tripp, 1988] is written in the first person. Molly is the first person in the book. The first sentence says: "Molly McIntire and her friend Susan stood at the bus stop waiting for the city bus to come and take them home." Her name is the first word in the book. Molly is a very nice girl. I trust her. I believe everything she says. I know this because I read *Meet Molly* and *Molly's Surprise*. I know that everything Molly says is the truth.

Clearly, Anita was really confused about first-person narratives. She wasn't the only one.

As Rhonda reflected on her minilesson, she realized that her mentor text might not have been accessible to all of her students, especially the struggling learners. Yes, they had participated in a shared reading of the text, but that lesson had taken place weeks ago. They had read one chapter in *Seedfolks* as a whole group, but only once. That reading was highly scaffolded. Although some students had read the book in its entirety, not everyone had. Not surprisingly, Anita was among those who hadn't read it. Anita had to devote energy to reading, comprehending, and even struggling with the book. Usually, Rhonda selected mentor texts that had been read and reread multiple times. Maybe she hadn't chosen the right mentor text for this lesson.

For the next day, Rhonda planned a review minilesson for the whole class, to be followed immediately by a small-group follow-up lesson for Anita and three other students—Jonelle, Andre, and Davion. For the small-group follow-up lesson, she selected the picture book *Those Shoes* (Boelts, 2009). The book is written at a third-grade reading level, easily accessible to everyone in the group, and it can be read in about 15 minutes.

First came the whole-class minilesson reviewing the concept of point of view. This time, she used the picture book *The True Story of the Three Little Pigs* (Scieszka, 1996), again emphasizing how the perspective of the narrator shapes the story. The class made an anchor chart showing that books written in the first person use the pronouns *I, me, my, we, our,* and *us*. Books written in the third person use the pronouns *he, she, his, hers, they, their,* and *them*. Then she sent the students off to do their independent reading.

Next came the small-group session with Anita, Jonelle, Andre, and Davion. She paired them up and asked them to read *Those Shoes*. While they were reading, Rhonda conducted conferences. After enough time had passed to allow them to complete their reading, she returned to the small group and asked them to discuss the story.

Everyone in the group was sympathetic to Jeremy's plight. They had all, at one time, wanted something badly but hadn't been able to get it because it was too expensive. Rhonda asked, "Who is telling the story?" The students easily identified Jeremy as the narrator. Jonelle commented that she didn't know the main character's name until the seventh page, when the counselor called him Jeremy.

Rhonda called the group's attention to the anchor chart and asked, "What is the point of view of this book?"

The group quickly responded, "First person."

"How does the fact that Jeremy is telling the story affect how we understand it?" Rhonda asked. Davion conjectured that maybe Jeremy had exaggerated some things because he had been so obsessed with the shoes. In particular, Davion thought that Nate probably hadn't gone to the bathroom seven times in one day; he doubted that the teacher would have permitted it. Andre thought that the shoes the counselor had given Jeremy probably weren't so bad and that the whole class probably hadn't laughed at him.

Rhonda told the group that there were two characters in the story who had different perspectives about the shoes. The students immediately identified Jeremy and his grandmother. Rhonda displayed a blank T-chart and asked the students to explain how Jeremy felt about the shoes, how the grandmother felt about the shoes, and the thoughts behind the feelings of each.

The students replied that Jeremy wanted the shoes more than anything. He wanted to be like everyone else; he did not want to be different. Rhonda asked them to find evidence in the text to support that idea. Anita pointed out that he was willing to walk around in shoes that were too small and hurt his feet just to fit in. She told about a time when she had outgrown her shoes but had tried to put them on anyway, and how much it had hurt. Similarly, Jonelle pointed out that Jeremy was willing to buy shoes that were too small. Davion said that he dreamed about the shoes. Anita pointed out that he was keeping track of who was getting the shoes.

From the grandmother's point of view, the students reported that she thought it was more important for Jeremy to have boots and that the shoes cost too much money. She thought that having money for things that they really needed, such as food and rent, was more important than cool shoes. Andre found a passage that said, "There's no room for 'want' around here, just 'need.'" Jonelle pointed out that Jeremy's grandmother was not even willing to spend $2.50 on shoes that were too small.

Rhonda recorded all the information about the contrasting perspectives on the T-chart. Then she asked, "Who is right?" After a lively discussion, the students agreed that no one was right or wrong. Jeremy and his grandmother just had different perspectives.

Rhonda returned to the question, "How does the fact that Jeremy is telling the story affect our understanding of the story?" The students were able to explain that it was a good idea to have Jeremy tell the story. It helped them understand how much he wanted the shoes. Since the story was told in the first person, the reader knows all of Jeremy's thoughts and feelings. Anita said, "If someone else told the story, we wouldn't know that he dreamed about the shoes or that when he wrote his spelling words, all the words looked like shoes. Jeremy is the only one who knows that." It was clear to Rhonda that Anita now understood how a story told in the first person affects the reader's understanding of the story.

Rhonda asked the students to revisit their journal entries from the previous day and reconsider what they had written. That evening, when she read Anita's reader response journal, she found this:

> *Changes for Molly* is written in the third person. The book used *she* and *they* when it was talking about the characters. The only time that the word *I* was used, it was in quotation marks. That shows that Molly was talking but not telling the story. This story took place long ago. I think it is a good idea to have the story in the third person to help the reader understand that Molly lived long ago and someone else has to tell her story.

Rhonda was satisfied with Anita's response. She was convinced that Anita had a basic understanding of point of view.

Rhonda is a reflective teacher. She knows that every lesson she teaches is an opportunity to help her become a better teacher. What did Rhonda learn about teaching struggling learners from this lesson?

- Struggling learners need the opportunity to practice a new concept using a book at their independent reading level, or even an easier book. The goal of the lesson is to learn the new concept. All of the students' energy needs to be devoted to learning the concept, not problem solving the text. Use easy books to teach new concepts.
- Stay current with students' reader response journals. Rhonda makes a point of reading the struggling learners' journals daily.
- Students, especially struggling learners, often require more than one minilesson to learn a new concept.
- Co-construct and support students in using anchor charts to bolster their learning.
- When struggling learners are confused about a concept, intervene as soon as possible. Anita thought "first person" was the first character to appear in a book. It was critical that Rhonda corrected the misconception soon enough to prevent Anita from having it become ingrained.

In review, when you have evidence that the struggling learners in your class are confused about a concept, plan to teach a second (review) minilesson accompanied by a small-group follow-up lesson. You might find that students who are not usually identified as struggling learners will experience confusions or misconceptions at one time or another. When reteaching a concept becomes necessary, plan to do so as soon as possible, so the students will not develop ingrained bad habits or solidify confusions. During the workshop period, teach a small-group lesson to those students who are confused. Use a text written at the students' independent reading level or easier. Include reading, writing, and talking in the lesson. Give the students an opportunity to apply the concept independently to ensure that they really understand it.

Section Three

CLASSROOM TEACHER AND INTERVENTIONIST COLLABORATION

Do you remember the pushmi-pullyu from the Dr. Dolittle books? He (she?) is a llama-like animal with two heads that face in opposite directions. Whenever the pushmi-pullyu tries to go somewhere, well . . . I'm sure you can imagine what happens. Students receiving intervention services must often feel like the pushmi-pullyu.

These are students who can be somewhat confused about the reading and writing processes. Unfortunately, their teachers are unwittingly pulling them (or pushing them) in different directions. The classroom teacher talks about "Bossy *R*" and "Sneaky *E*." However, the interventionist talks about "*R*-Controlled *A*" and "Silent *E*." The befuddled students haven't quite figured out that both teachers are talking about the same thing.

The classroom teacher encourages a student to "sound it out" when she encounters an unknown word. However, the interventionist encourages the student to skip the word and keep on reading to the end of the sentence before going back to the troublesome word and thinking about what would make sense, using the letter cues to help.

During writing instruction, the classroom teacher insists that the student should use her best handwriting, make sure that all the words are spelled correctly, and use correct punctuation. This entails always having a dictionary handy to check spellings. However, the interventionist tells the student to prewrite, make a sketch or a web, and then do a quick write and develop it into a draft. At that point the student should go back to the draft and work on word choice, the opening, the ending, and the transitions. Only when the writing sounds just the way she wants it should she perform an edit that includes checking the spelling and punctuation.

It is no wonder that students working with interventionists sometimes struggle to make progress! Teacher-interventionist collaboration is critical for all of the following reasons:

- Most intervention groups meet for no more than 9 percent of the school day. The interventionist cannot be effective without detailed information about the overwhelming majority of the student's school experience.
- Intervention instruction is likely to be the most intensive, targeted instruction of the day. The classroom teacher needs to know what is happening there so that she can address the objectives of the intervention in individual conferences and small-group instruction.
- The goal of intervention is for the student to be successful in the classroom. It doesn't help for the student to ace his intervention lessons if he still flounders in the classroom.
- Teachers and interventionists both want their students to succeed. But this mutual goal can be achieved effectively only if they work together.

NO TIME
FOR COLLABORATION

Marnie, a literacy interventionist, double-checked her notes. She had it right. Andy, a fifth grader, was indeed reading *Poppy* (Avi, 2005). Andy kept calling the main character Bobby instead of Poppy. He seemed really confused about the plot, the characters, and, well . . . just about everything. He couldn't seem to recall even the most basic details of the book, even though his reading log indicated that he had completed the first four chapters. Initially, Marnie had thought that the book might be a bit out of Andy's reach. But she had listened while he read the first couple of pages, and he had seemed very comfortable doing so. There was also good reason to believe that he was very motivated to read the book. *Poppy* is an animal fantasy, and Andy loves animal fantasies; he had devoured books such as the Catwings series (LeGuin), *The Mouse and the Motorcycle* (Cleary, 1990), and *Stuart Little* (White, 2005). So what could the problem be?

At the next session, Marnie asked Andy what he thought Poppy could do to elude Mr. Ocax. (Mr. Ocax is an owl and Poppy is a mouse.)

He said, "I think Bobby should become invisible."

Marnie sputtered, "What do you mean? The mouse's name is Poppy, not Bobby. How can Poppy become invisible?" Andy just sat there looking confused. At that point, Marnie decided that the only viable choice was to halt the conference and send Andy off to reread Chapter 4—a chapter that he reportedly had finished.

After that session, Marnie sat there wondering what could be going on with Andy. He had always been such a hardworking student. He had started intervention group two years below grade level. But that gap had been whittled down to a single year, and until fairly recently, Marnie had considered it to be a realistic goal for him to place out of intervention by the end of the school year. Now Marnie realized that that goal might be in jeopardy. Although her schedule was jam-packed, she would have to find some time to talk to Andy's teacher. Unfortunately, her school did not build any time into the school day for collaboration. The administrators said they did not have the staff available to cover classrooms. If any collaboration was to be done, it would have to be on the teacher's own time.

At the end of the school day, Marnie traded her bus duty with one of her fellow interventionists so that she could try to catch Andy's teacher before she left for the day. When she reached Andy's classroom, the teacher, Liz, was standing there with her coat on, stuffing papers into a tote bag.

Marnie said, "Hi, Liz. Can I talk to you about Andy for a minute?"

"I'm really sorry," Liz replied. "My grad class starts in forty minutes. I'm doing a presentation today. I need to get there to set up."

"When can we talk?" Marnie asked.

"I don't know," Liz said. "Why don't you send me an email? I really have to run. I can't take the time to pull out my calendar right now."

Marnie watched Liz rush out the door. Then she went back to her office and sent Liz an email. She received a reply the next morning offering three possible meeting times, but all of them conflicted with Marnie's schedule because of one of her groups or a team meeting. She could trade duties with someone, but rescheduling a team meeting or a group was almost impossible. The school's master schedule was a house of cards; trying to move one thing would cause everything else to come tumbling down. Marnie replied to the email with some suggestions of her own. The emails flew back and forth for the next several days. Finally, she and Liz agreed to meet for 10 minutes before the next faculty meeting. Marnie didn't think that 10 minutes would be long enough, but at this point, she'd take what she could get.

Marnie explained to Liz that Andy had been making fairly good progress until recently. She had brought along his reading log, his response journal, his running records, and her anecdotal notes, even though she knew that there was no time for Liz to really look at them. Marnie described Andy's recent lapses—the inability to retain basic information about the story, the superficial response-journal entries, and calling the main character Bobby instead of Poppy.

Liz said, "That's funny. He keeps calling the main character in our class novel Poppy instead of Bobby."

"Your class novel? I thought you conducted a reading workshop. Aren't your students reading self-selected books?"

"Oh, they still have their self-selected books," Liz replied. "But we are reading *Things Not Seen* [Clements, 2006] as a class novel, too. I met with Cindy and Lena [the other fifth-grade teachers], and we decided that it would help them get ready for middle school. This book addresses the social issues that kids face in middle school and high school."

Marnie then realized that Andy was trying to read three books at the same time. Marnie has a hard time doing that herself even though she is an avid, accomplished adult reader. Andy, as a struggling reader, was being asked to remember the story line and characters of three different books simultaneously. No wonder the poor boy was confused! The principal called the meeting to order, and they had to stop talking.

Marnie was frustrated. Why hadn't she known that the fifth grade was doing a whole-class novel study? If she had known that, she could have made some adjustments. Maybe she could have given Andy a collection of short stories to read, such as *Every Living Thing* (Rylant, 1996)—or maybe some magazine articles. She realized that it was very important to find a way to regularly communicate with teachers to avoid these situations.

After the teachers' meeting, Marnie tried to corner Liz for a minute to schedule another meeting. Liz said, "I'm sorry, Marnie. I simply can't right now. I have to go and set up a science experiment before the kids come in."

Marnie said, "But we need to find a way to collaborate if we are going to help Andy."

Liz sighed and said, "Andy is not my only student. I have twenty-four others with a wide range of abilities, needs, and learning styles. I have to teach them everything, not just reading. If I don't get back to my room right now, I am going to have a chaotic morning because I'm not ready for them." Once again, Marnie watched Liz rush out the door.

Marnie sighed, too. She had a caseload of 32 students, seven more than Liz, across three different grade levels. She had to submit weekly progress monitoring reports for each of these students and prepare for and attend monthly intervention conferences. She had to administer diagnostic assessments to all the students about whom teachers expressed concern and universal screening assessments to newly enrolled students. In addition, the literacy team was responsible for all school literacy events, such as Family Reading Night and the book sale, as well as for maintaining the school book room and the professional library. Since she didn't have a regular class, she was also scheduled for bus duty, lunch duty, and recess duty. She had all of these responsibilities, yet she was motivated to find time to meet. Marnie was not willing to surrender yet. At least Liz had responded to her emails. She'd try sending her another email.

During lunch with the two other interventionists, she told them about the difficulty in finding time to collaborate with Liz. She told them that she was going to try to collaborate via email. The school counselor was in the lunchroom and overheard the conversation. He told them that they should never send any information about students over the Internet. It is not completely secure, and there was a risk of violating confidentiality. Now Marnie was back to the drawing board.

That evening, Marnie's five-year-old son gave her his "home-school folder." Marnie and all of the other kindergarten parents were told to be on the lookout for the "home-school folder" every day. It contained flyers, notices, notes from the teacher, corrected papers, and homework. Marnie had to empty the folder of corrected papers and flyers. She signed anything that needed to be signed and returned it to the folder. If she wanted to send a note to the teacher, she would put it in the home-school folder. Marnie put her son's homework aside until after his snack and 30 minutes of media time. That evening, when she was returning the folder to her son's backpack, the idea struck her. She and Liz could have a "home-school folder." They wouldn't have to find a time to meet. They could communicate in writing, and Andy could be the courier.

For Marnie to have any hope that Liz would read the information in the folder, she would have to be succinct. Liz wouldn't read pages and pages. As a matter of fact, she probably wouldn't even read a whole page. Marnie was certainly willing to keep Liz informed and eventually hoped to persuade Liz to use this information to provide more effective classroom instruction for Andy. But her immediate goal was information flow in the other direction, i.e., for Liz to keep her apprised of happenings in the classroom, which would enable her to greatly improve the effectiveness of her intervention sessions with Andy. However, getting Liz to write back would be a real challenge. It would have to be easy and to the point. Then she thought about the form she had filled out to put in her son's home-school folder. She had checked a couple of boxes and written a few phrases, yet it communicated all that the teacher needed to know about her son's reading experience that evening.

She could create a form. Liz would only have to check boxes and write short phrases, and then Marnie would have the needed information! The next morning, Marnie started working on the form. She shared a draft of the form with the other members of the literacy team. They reviewed it and gave feedback, including some of their own ideas for improving it. A couple of the other interventionists expressed interest in using it, too, once Marnie finished developing it. After several drafts, she was finally ready to start using the form.

Marnie gave the folder to Andy and asked him to give it to Liz. The folder contained both the form completed by Marnie and a blank form with a sticky note attached requesting that Liz complete it, put it back in the folder, and return the folder via Andy. The next day, Andy came to intervention class without the folder. He also didn't bring it the following day or for the rest of the week. Marnie was about to give up, but early the next week, Andy came to class with the folder. Marnie peeked inside and was delighted to see that Liz had completed the form.

Liz and Marnie developed a routine of completing the form at least once a week. Andy eventually asked about it, and Marnie explained the purpose of the folder. During that day's session, Andy discovered a way to help himself keep track of the characters in his novel. Andy suggested that Marnie write that on the form. Marnie said, "Why don't you write it on the form yourself?" Andy did. From then on, the folder became a three-way communication between Marnie, Liz, and Andy. Andy took responsibility for filling out the parts that were obvious to him, such as the title of the book he was reading. In addition to all the other uses for the folder, it provided Marnie with another method to measure Andy's progress. She knew that Andy truly understood the lessons being taught when he could fill in the "strategy focus" and "word study" portions of the form.

The collaboration folder continued to expand and evolve. In addition to the completed form, Marnie would occasionally add a copy of her anecdotal notes or a running record that denoted a change in Andy's strategy use. Liz included standard-size copies of her class anchor charts in the folder whenever the class created new ones. Marnie noticed that Andy found the anchor charts extremely helpful, so she had him affix them into the "resources pages" section of his reader response journal.

Eventually, the entire literacy team and some of the special education resource teachers adopted the collaboration folder. Some teachers and interventionists even took the concept a step further—they began communicating through a collaboration log. The collaboration log was simply a spiral notebook. The teacher and interventionist wrote observations about their student in the notebook and put it in each other's mailboxes rather than delivering it via student couriers. The collaboration log turned out to be a rich source of documentation at intervention meetings.

The collaboration folder had a very positive effect on Andy's progress. Marnie used it to improve her intervention sessions with him right from the beginning—and to her delight, Liz eventually also started to use it to modify some aspects of Andy's classroom instruction. Thus, his intervention sessions and classroom instruction became progressively more aligned with each other. Among other changes, the kinds of inconsistent terminology and contradictory instructional approaches that are described above were eliminated. Once Andy started to receive instruction that was coordinated between his classroom and his intervention group with a common goal, mastery occurred at a much faster rate.

Teacher-Interventionist Collaboration Sheet

Name_____ Date_____

Instructional Goal: _____

_____

Strategy Focus: _____

_____

Word Study Focus: _____

_____

Resources Used: _____

_____

_____

_____

Observable Behaviors: _____

_____

Notes:

CLASSROOM AND INTERVENTION SESSION OBSERVATION

Lorna couldn't believe what she was hearing. She was attending the first quarterly intervention conference of the school year. Tanya, Malik's teacher, was describing his behaviors in the classroom. Malik was a fourth grader who was new at their school this year. He was a definite outlier on the school's universal screening assessment. His fluency rate was at the first-grade level. The diagnostic assessment revealed that he was a proficient decoder, yet he had an underdeveloped vocabulary and exhibited difficulty with comprehension. Tanya described a student who rarely completed assignments, got failing grades on classroom tests, was reading level J books, and had only two completed books listed on his reading log in the first quarter of the school year.

Lorna had been working with Malik for eight weeks now. She worked with him in a group with three other children. She had had the opportunity to observe him closely and document his reading and writing behaviors. Malik was cooperative and engaged. He loved informational books on "boy topics" such as snakes, frogs, spiders, sharks, and volcanoes. He had read every single Nic Bishop book that Lorna had in her collection. He routinely filled pages in his response journal. Just the day before, Lorna had taken a running record of Malik reading Nic Bishop's *Lizards* (2010), a level N book. He had read it with 90 percent accuracy. Although 90 percent is not independent and not even quite instructional, it paints a drastically different picture from what she was now hearing. The child Tanya was describing was definitely not Malik!

Maintaining her professional demeanor, Lorna gave her report. She provided substantial documentation to support her assertions about Malik. More than 10 running records (two of them on benchmark books), a reader response journal, four fluency snapshots, and pages of anecdotal notes showed a student on a definite upward trajectory. The only documents that Tanya had brought to the meeting were her grade book and Malik's reading log. Lorna stole a glance at Tanya and saw that she was poring over Malik's reader response journal. She couldn't tear her eyes away from the pages and pages that he had written about the books he had read.

Tanya finally looked up and said to Lorna, "How did you do this? I can't get him to do anything. I would love to see what you are doing."

Lorna replied, "Come anytime." The committee decided that Malik should continue to receive intervention services at the same rate, and the meeting was adjourned.

The next morning, there was a note in Lorna's mailbox from the principal asking her to stop by the office before she went to her classroom. The principal told her that the case manager was concerned about the discrepancy between Malik's performances in the classroom and the intervention group. He said he had heard that Lorna was open to being observed by classroom teachers. Lorna assured him that she indeed was open to the idea. He asked if she thought the other interventionists would feel the same way. Lorna guessed that they probably would and suggested that he ask them. He then thanked her and told her he would work on it.

Lorna was right. The other interventionists loved the idea of hosting visits from classroom teachers. Within two weeks, Lorna's school held an Intervention Class Open House. The school hired two substitute teachers to provide coverage for the regular classrooms. Teachers were invited to sign up to participate. Participating classroom teachers needed to agree to

- prepare activities to engage the students in their class-rooms for the duration of the observation,
- write a reflection on what was learned, and
- write a plan for applying what was learned.

Lorna and the other interventionists were eagerly looking forward to sharing their work with their colleagues.

Unfortunately, the project was not well received. Only 40 percent of the classroom teachers opted to participate. The regular classroom teachers did not like the "assignment" that was attached to the observation. Some teachers were offended by what they perceived as an assumption that they were not doing an adequate job teaching literacy. Some teachers reported that they did not want to "steal instructional time" from the other students in their classrooms for the intervention students. As it was, they were already required to attend quarterly conferences for the intervention students.

To make matters worse, the teachers who did participate did not exactly give the experience rave reviews. Their reflections were defensive. They talked about how small the intervention groups were. In their own classrooms, most of the small groups were composed of six students. Some teachers even had small groups consisting of as many as eight students. They talked about the quiet setting. The intervention teacher did not have to be concerned about keeping 20 other students quietly engaged in another activity while she was working with the small group. They talked about the furniture, materials, and equipment that were in the intervention rooms that they did not have in their own classrooms. They talked about the classroom displays and the organization of student resources. However, there were very few comments about the actual instruction.

The literacy committee met to discuss the apparent failure of the project. The principal attended the meeting. He responded to the criticism about "the assignment." He reported that he had used district professional development funds to pay for the substitute teachers. It was the district's policy that teachers must write reflections and a plan for applying what was learned when professional development funds were used. These reports had to be submitted to the district office. The interventionists were dismayed by the classroom teachers' lack of focus on instruction. Nobody on the committee wanted to abandon the project, but to make it viable, they would clearly have to come up with a revision that would be more attractive to the classroom teachers.

The committee came up with the idea of reversing the observation. Instead of the classroom teachers visiting the intervention class, the interventionists would observe their students during regular classroom literacy instruction. This observation would require no substitute teachers. Although this eliminated the district's requirement for "the assignment," the interventionists decided to do it anyway for two different reasons. First, they wanted to avoid possible resentment from the classroom teachers over perceived asymmetry in the arrangement. Second, and perhaps more important, was the feeling of the interventionists that a written reflection on what was learned and a plan for applying it had inherent educational merit that would improve the value of the experience.

Since they were invested in the project, they were more than willing to make this extra effort. The case manager had a great idea. Instead of calling it an "observation," they would call it a "visit." The interventionists were going to visit their students during sessions of regular classroom instruction.

There were some rumblings when the announcement was made. Some teachers complained that they structured their small-group instruction around the time when the intervention students were gone. These students did not have very much reading stamina. How would they keep them engaged for an entire 90-minute literacy block? The union representative was concerned about exceeding the contracted number of observations for teachers in good standing. The principal reiterated that the interventionists were not conducting observations. They were simply visiting their students during regular instruction to see how they were applying their specialized instruction.

The "visits" were a bit tense. Some teachers were visibly nervous. One teacher asked to see what the interventionist was writing. Some teachers "showed off" by having their students perform elaborately produced readers' theater presentations.

Some teachers presented the interventionists with formal, typed lesson plans. In spite of the tensions, the interventionists found the experience insightful and worthwhile.

Lorna watched as Malik spent 30 minutes trying to select an independent-reading book—a third of the literacy block time! Lorna considered intervening, but she wanted to see what he'd do on his own. Tanya was busy working with small groups and conducting conferences. She didn't seem to notice how long Malik was spending looking for a book. When he finally settled on a book, it was *Gorilla Doctors: Saving Endangered Great Apes* (Turner, 2005). Although it was just the kind of book that Malik would love, it was far too difficult.

Later, Lorna looked up the book and learned that it was level Y, significantly above Malik's independent-reading level. If this was representative of the books that Malik typically selected, it was no wonder he had completed only two books during the first quarter of the school year. He would have to work really hard to read such a book. She would have to teach him to select "just right" books. Selecting "just right" books wasn't an issue in the intervention room. Malik knew that he should pick books with yellow or green dots.

At the next literacy committee meeting, Lorna discovered that her experience during her visit to Tanya's classroom was fairly typical. All of the interventionists learned some bits of important information about their students by watching them during regular classroom instruction. One interventionist was gratified to report that she saw one of her students using a strategy that the student had learned during an intervention session. Another interventionist reported that a subtly delivered cue was enough to get one of her students back on track when things were going awry with the student's reading. The interventionists talked about the classroom teachers' use of language and organizational practices that they could apply in the intervention sessions that would help make the transition from the classroom to the intervention room more fluid for their students.

However, the interventionists also noticed more ways that they could support classroom teachers. For example, some of the classroom teachers seemed to be confused by certain instructional practices. The interventionists believed that if the class-room teachers could see these practices applied appropriately, it would help clear up some of the confusion. How could this be done in such a way that the teachers would feel supported rather than criticized? This could certainly not be accomplished if the interactions didn't continue, so the first objective was to find some way to keep the visits going. The interventionists decided to highlight all of the wonderful things that they had learned by visiting the regular classrooms.

At the next faculty meeting, the interventionists presented kudos (both verbal and Kudos candy bars!) to each teacher they had visited. The classroom teachers were both delighted by the recognition and intrigued by what they were learning about what was happening in other classrooms. The fact that "the lit-eracy experts" had learned something from visiting their class-rooms helped them relax about the idea of hosting visits.

Lorna's school revamped the whole Intervention Room Open House process. The first change was that the visits now went in both directions; the classroom teachers visited the inter-vention classes, and the interventionists visited the classrooms. The second change was that whichever teacher was visiting the other one's class would complete a pre-visit form (yes, more assignments). The form would provide an objective for the visit and a rationale for the objective.

For example, in that first quarterly intervention meeting, Tanya had said that she wanted to learn what Lorna was doing to support the volume of writing that Malik was producing. Although she had been among the minority of classroom teachers who had attended the original Intervention Class Open House, she felt that she had more to learn along those lines and wanted to visit Malik's intervention class again. Conversely, during Lorna's first visit to Tanya's room, she saw that Malik was having difficulty finding "just right" books. She said that she would like a follow-up visit to see if Malik was doing a better job of self-selecting books.

When a teacher received a completed pre-visit form, she would make sure that the instruction for the day would address the visiting teacher's objective. When Tanya visited Malik's intervention class, Lorna would make sure that the day's lesson included a writing component. When Lorna visited Malik's regular classroom, Tanya would make sure that Malik was selecting a book that day.

After a bumpy start, the visits became a staple in the school's professional development program. Once each quarter, the interventionists visited their students' classrooms, and the classroom teachers visited one of their students' intervention sessions. The visits became less tense and a lot more interactive. Lorna now feels free to get up and coach Malik through a book selection in his regular classroom. The other interventionists no longer have to surreptitiously prompt students who are struggling with a text.

The big winner in the process is the students—both the intervention students and their on-grade-level peers. Their teachers are getting job-embedded professional development on how to support the struggling learners as well as clarification on instructional literacy strategies for all of the students, such as guided reading, effective conferences, and prompting students. With both groups of teachers working together, the intervention students benefit from aligned instructional programs.

Visitation Request Form

Student's Name

Room	Grade
Intervention Visit?	Classroom Visit?

Visit's Objective

Objective Rationale

Requested by

Classroom Visitation Form

Date:

Visit Objective:

What is the teacher doing?	What are students doing?

Questions, additional notes

COLLABORATIVE GRADE-LEVEL TEAM MEETINGS

Weekly grade-level team meetings have become a staple in many schools. All of the students in the classes at a specific grade level are scheduled for a "special" class (for example, music, art, technology, or physical education), and their teachers use the time to meet. In these meetings, the teachers plan together, reflect, and problem-solve instructional and management issues. Most teams have a designated meeting facilitator and a recording secretary. In many schools, these roles rotate among the teachers on the team. Each meeting has an agenda, which often consists of topics that were decided upon at the end of the previous meeting. If the time is used appropriately, grade-level team meetings can be powerful professional development tools. Unfortunately, the team member who is usually missing from these meetings is the interventionist who supports the struggling learners at that grade level.

In the 2011–2012 school year, Washington School decided to address the issue of "the missing team member." A school schedule was devised to enable the interventionists who support the struggling learners at specific grade levels to attend up to two grade-level team meetings each month. To ensure productivity, each weekly meeting has a particular focus: literacy, mathematics, or content instruction. A special monthly meeting uses the data wall. Each student in the school has a card on the data wall. The card is placed on the wall to indicate the student's current level of achievement. The interventionists always, of course, attend the literacy-focused meetings, and they also try to attend the meetings in which teachers move cards on the data wall.

Ginny was about to attend the third-grade-level team meeting for the third time this school year. She is the interventionist for all three groups of third-grade students who need additional support, and she also has one second-grade intervention group and one fourth-grade intervention group. Washington School was able to fit the team meetings into the interventionists' schedules by having each interventionist focus on a single grade level and, if necessary, also take an overflow of students from the adjoining grade levels. Ginny tries to attend a second-grade- and a fourth-grade-level team meeting at least once a quarter, but she mostly relies on the other interventionists to keep her informed about the second and fourth grades. She also makes sure to read the notes from those meetings.

Ginny's first two third-grade-level team meetings had focused on data analysis. With the support of the literacy coach, the teachers had closely examined the results of the school's universal screening assessment. They had identified students in need of a diagnostic assessment and had created cards for the reading data wall. They also analyzed the results to see what the assessment could tell them about the literacy instruction at their school.

Today's meeting was to be the first of several to address the topic of "thinking within the text." The school's universal screening assessment evaluates students' ability to think within, beyond, and about text. This organization of text processing was new for Washington School's teachers. The universal screening assessment data suggested that many of their students struggled in one or more of these areas. The third-grade team wanted to examine their practices to see if they could find ways to better support students in thinking within, beyond, and about the text, starting with the "within" component.

"Thinking within the text" addresses word solving, monitoring, searching, summarizing, fluency, and adjusting. These topics are especially relevant to the work that Ginny does with her intervention students. Many of them plow through the text, focusing on getting to the end of the book or passage with little regard for monitoring, adjusting, or searching. When Ginny asks her students to summarize, they often either retell the passage with so many minor details that the main idea is lost in the sea of words, or their description is so general that it says nothing substantive about what happened in the passage (for example, "It was about pandas.").

"Thinking within the text" is too broad a topic for a single 45-minute meeting, so the team had decided to focus on monitoring comprehension in today's meeting. In preparation, between the previous meeting and this one, the team members had taught lessons in their classrooms on monitoring comprehension, and they were supposed to bring something to this meeting to share with their colleagues about these lessons. Ginny was headed to the meeting armed with some of her students' running records, some of their reader response journals, and a handout on a strategy that she uses to help students monitor their comprehension. She knew that it was unlikely that she would be able to talk about all three of these items in this meeting, so she entered the room prepared to present whichever one turned out to be most relevant to the discussion.

The meeting started the way it always does, with "celebrations." Each team member told a short anecdote or quickly shared a sample of student work that celebrated a breakthrough or some evidence of student progress. Celebrations serve two purposes. It is easy to become bogged down in "negatives" such as demands from the administration, difficult parents and students, or feeling overwhelmed. Celebrations spotlight the "positives" and remind the teachers that some things are going right in their classrooms. The other purpose of celebrations is to share successful strategies with the team. If something is working well in one classroom, chances are good that it will also work well in the other classrooms.

Then the teachers dived right into the main topic of the meeting. They began sharing strategies for explicitly teaching students to monitor their comprehension. Myrna, a 20-year veteran, swears by the Say Something and Directed Reading Thinking Activity (DRTA) strategies. In the Say Something strategy, students read to a predetermined place in the text, then stop and "say something" to a designated partner. In the DRTA strategy, students make a prediction after reading the title of a passage, and then stop at predetermined places to revise or confirm their prediction. The students must provide evidence from the text to support the revision or confirmation. At the meeting, Myrna distributed handouts describing these two strategies.

Irena brought an anchor chart that she had started with her class titled "What to Do When Things Go Wrong." So far, the chart had four items:

1. Stop and think—does the text make sense?
2. If it does, keep reading.
3. If it doesn't, go back to find where things fell apart.
4. Determine what caused things to fall apart.
   • Was there a word that I could not read?
   • Was there a word that I didn't know the meaning of?

Irena's students were still working on what could go wrong. Irena said that she planned for the anchor chart to eventually list the steps that can be used to fix things. She reported that the chart was being developed through a series of reading minilessons and focus lessons. The day before, she had used *The Day of Ahmed's Secret* (Heide, 1995) in a shared reading. Each of her students had been given a red octagon affixed to a tongue depressor. The students were asked to hold up their stop sign when their comprehension was breaking down.

Everyone liked Irena's lesson and her chart. They all thought that it was a really good idea to create anchor charts with their students. Irena promised to give them a list of the books that she had used so far for her minilessons and focus lessons.

Chloe found a lesson on the Internet that had been developed to help students monitor their comprehension. The lesson used an informational text containing several elements that were specifically designed to interfere with comprehension, including a nonsense word, a modern convenience (although it was a historical piece), and an awkwardly constructed sentence. At least at those three points, students should naturally pause if they are effectively monitoring their comprehension. Chloe's students were instructed to read the passage independently and to put a question mark when their comprehension broke down. Then the classroom read the piece together on the smartboard and shared their thinking. At the meeting, Chloe distributed copies of the article to everyone for possible use in their own classrooms.

Then it was Ginny's turn. She first distributed copies of one of the running records of Nicole, a third grader. She told the team that a running record can be used as a window to a student's comprehension monitoring. She pointed out a place where Nicole had self-corrected an error. In the initial reading, Nicole had relied on visual cues to read the word. When the sentence hadn't made sense to her, she had gone back, reread the word more carefully, and solved it. Ginny also pointed out other places in the running record where Nicole had gone back and reread. In some cases, she had reread the phrase containing the word to solve it, probably using meaning cues. When the word was particularly difficult, the process of solving it had taken so much of Nicole's energy and attention that she had forgotten its context. In such cases, after solving the word, Nicole had needed to go back and reread the entire sentence to maintain comprehension of the text. Ginny told the teachers that all of the rereading was a good indication that Nicole was indeed monitoring her comprehension.

Not all of Ginny's students were as diligent. She next distributed copies of one of the running records of Omar, another third grader. Omar seldom self-corrected. He was almost always satisfied to let a completely nonsensical sentence remain as he had read it. He overrelied on visual cues.

When Omar had finished reading the selection, Ginny had asked him, "Show me where things got confusing or you had to do some work." But Omar had not acknowledged any difficulty reading and understanding the text. Finally, when Ginny had asked him to retell the passage, he had been able to provide only very general information. Obviously, Omar was not monitoring his comprehension. From Ginny's observation of his reading behaviors and the running record analysis, she theorized that it was because he had little metacognition. Omar had yet to understand that reading is thinking. He believed that reading is just getting the words right. Ginny told the team members that it is not enough to know that a particular student would benefit from comprehension instruction. If you can pinpoint where things are going wrong with the student, you can help much more effectively by providing targeted support.

Anna, the literacy coach, always has the last word at team meetings. She asked the team to decide specifically what they would work on in their classrooms before the next meeting. The team chose to continue with the comprehension monitoring lessons. They also decided to do running records with the students in their lowest group to provide more focused instruction for them. In addition, each teacher was going to co-create anchor charts in the classroom and share the charts with Ginny.

Anna encouraged the teachers to consider providing comprehension instruction in small groups in addition to the usual whole-class instruction. She reminded them to use easy books when teaching strategies. This enables the students to devote their energy and attention to the strategy, not the reading. She asked if anyone wanted to be videotaped to help them reflect on their instruction or to share with the team in an upcoming meeting. Irena volunteered to be videotaped while working further on the anchor chart. Finally, Anna promised to compile a collection of picture books and other short texts that would be good to use for teaching comprehension monitoring.

For the next meeting, they would share what they had learned from their running record analysis, report on their current progress on comprehension monitoring, and watch the video of Irena's anchor chart lesson.

Ginny was delighted that the classroom teachers now seemed to recognize the value of taking and analyzing running records; they had been resistant to this idea in the past. She was also pleased that she could now regularly attend grade-level team meetings. The information gained from these meetings has helped her align her intervention instruction to what's happening in the classroom. She is already planning to reinforce the classroom lessons by working on comprehension monitoring in intervention lessons, too. The students are the big winners from this arrangement.

A FINAL WORD ON TEACHER-AND-INTERVENTIONIST COLLABORATION

I've shared three ways in which teachers and interventionists can collaborate:

- a collaboration folder or log, especially when no time has been allocated for collaboration,
- quarterly observations in the classroom and the intervention room, and
- full participation of all professionals working with students in a grade-level team meeting.

Of course, a combination of any and all of these options can also be employed—the more, the better! Two of these three strategies require administration support and cooperation.

Make the case for built-in collaboration time to your school administrator. Remind her that any future claims the school might make about overall achievement will ring hollow if the progress of the lowest-functioning students is poor. Dorn and Soffos (2011) say that we should strive for "seamless" instruction between the classroom and the intervention room. That means common instructional goals, common language, and common resources. We can find that common ground only if we can get together to talk, think, and reflect.

Administrators will sometimes say that there is no money for collaboration. Look at the examples provided here for ideas. Lorna's school used professional development funds to pay for the substitute teachers that made the observations possible. Most schools and school districts have a professional development line in their budget. School districts, on average, spend $4,360 per teacher per year for professional development (Miles et al., 2004). The cost of a substitute teacher ($75–$150 per day) is a mere 1.7–3.4 percent of that amount. There is still lots of money left over for conferences, workshops, graduate classes, and an on-site literacy coach. I suspect that time spent on mutual observation is more beneficial than those expensive, crowded, isolated, one-shot workshops, which also require a substitute teacher!

Washington School spent no money at all freeing the interventionists to attend team meetings. They simply reconfigured the intervention groups by focusing each interventionist on a specific grade level. As a result, each interventionist attends two grade-level team meetings each month. During any week in which the interventionist attends a grade-level team meeting, she does not meet with one of her groups. The missed group rotates so that each group ends up missing only an occasional session. Despite missed days because of school holidays, field trips, assemblies, and teacher and student absences, this leaves enough time in the schedule for each group to have 16–18 intervention sessions per month, which is the frequency that Washington School strives for.

The time spent in observations and collaborative team meetings results in markedly better instruction for struggling students in both the classroom and the intervention room. It is well worth giving up one intervention session per month for this purpose.

Conclusion

MONICA'S INTERVENTION STORY: A HAPPY ENDING?

Monica's intervention story *can* have a happy ending. We can make it happen by maximizing the instructional opportunities in the regular classroom. Intervention instruction is most successful when the student is fully engaged in appropriate instruction in the regular classroom, too. Here are five things that classroom teachers, interventionists, and administrators can do to ensure that Monica's story has a happy ending.

1. *Evaluate instructional materials and make adaptations to meet the needs of all students.*
Monica and all struggling learners need to have access to texts that they can actually read. Monica's classroom teacher complained that Monica doesn't seem to understand what she is reading when participating in content instruction. She could not correctly answer even factual-level questions about a chapter

that the class had just read in the textbook. I'm betting that is because Monica couldn't read the book.

Tyreese was failing social studies until the literacy coach intervened and put together differentiated text sets on the topic addressed in the textbook. Once Tyreese developed some background knowledge on the topic by reading easier books, he was able to negotiate the textbook chapter with the support of his classmates.

Allington (2002) said, "You can't learn much from books that you can't read." If your students can't read their textbooks, you can do something about it. Grade-level teams, with the support of the literacy coach and other literacy professionals in the school (interventionists, reading specialists, reading resource teachers, and so on), can develop differentiated text sets for the content-area topics studied at a grade level. It will take work, time, and probably a little money. This is certainly a worthy summer curriculum project. Why just "a little" money? Most schools allocate funds for textbooks, so the funding is already in place. We just have to think about using it differently. Textbooks can still be used as one of the resources for content instruction rather than as the entire instructional program. If schools would purchase group sets of textbooks (8–10 copies) instead of classroom sets of textbooks (20–30) and spend the balance of the textbook allocation on text sets, there would probably be sufficient funds available. There are even some leveled-books publishers that offer books on content topics that can be included in your text sets.

Both Monica and Tyreese were enrolled in intervention programs that were yielding positive results. Ideally, one day they will be able to successfully read their grade-level textbooks. Until then, let's make it possible for them to get the information even if they can't read the textbooks.

2. *Use a workshop model to shift from an emphasis on whole-group instruction to small-group, individual, and multilevel instruction.* There are no homogeneous classrooms. There will always be students at the ends of the continuum. Whenever a teacher presents an extended whole-class lesson (45 minutes) using a single

text, it is very likely that it is not within the reach of many of the students. Under these circumstances, it is hard to justify presenting one lesson after another in a whole-class format. Increase the number of lessons presented in small groups or individualized settings, or use multilevel materials.

Jamal was able to fully participate in the activities of his class's poetry unit once his teacher, Peter, gave him a poetry-embedded novel that he could read. Peter taught all of the lessons that he usually taught in the poetry unit using three poetry-embedded novels at different levels instead of just one, allowing all students to be engaged. Peter used all the grouping configurations while teaching this unit. He taught whole-class minilessons, met with small groups, and also met with individual students.

A workshop framework gives the teacher an opportunity to present information, demonstrate a strategy, or clarify a concept in a minilesson. Then the students get to practice or apply what was taught using resources that they can read. While all of the students are engaged in individual reading and writing, the teacher can follow up, reinforce, and extend the lesson with small groups and individuals.

Rhonda taught her whole class a lesson on point of view. However, Anita was confused about the concept, so Rhonda taught a follow-up lesson to a small group that included Anita during the workshop period. A classroom that uses a workshop framework is a great place for struggling learners to thrive.

Whole-group instruction can be ineffective if it is poorly planned, but you can make it productive and even powerful with advance thought and careful choices, especially when you use it to explicitly demonstrate reading and writing. Struggling learners benefit from explicit demonstrations of how reading and writing works. Teachers can employ instructional strategies such as interactive read-aloud, shared reading, and shared writing to help students truly understand how reading and writing works.

Sara helped her students move beyond the literal level in reading when she demonstrated making inferences using *Dear Mrs. LaRue* (Teague, 2002) using the interactive read-aloud instructional strategy. Since Sara was doing the reading, the students could devote their energy to learning the strategy.

Belinda's students wrote higher-quality argumentative essays after she engaged them in the shared writing of a persuasive letter. Again, Belinda did the actual writing. She took care of the conventions (spelling, punctuation, and grammar), freeing her students' attention and energy for the composition of the letter. After that powerful and motivating learning experience, her students went on to write notably improved argumentative essays.

Rhonda did a shared reading of a chapter in *Seedfolks* (Fleischman, 2004) to help her students see how an author can use words to help readers visualize. The benefits of this experience were twofold. Her students practiced visualizing from written text, and they applied what they learned from that lesson to their writing. They were better able to "show—not tell" after examining how Paul Fleischman did it.

Demonstration is at the heart of instruction. It is not effective to just tell students how to visualize, infer, argue, and describe. We have to show them.

3. *Build time into the school day for independent reading.*
Nothing improves reading like increasing the amount of reading that students are doing. The more they read, they better they'll get at reading. Although we'd all love it if our students read outside of school, many of them need to have the foundation laid in the classroom—especially struggling readers.

Series books are a great way to help students develop the reading habit. Spend the time necessary to match students with a series that they will love so that they can get the reading started—it's worth it. Once Dana got Jaden started on the Ricky Ricotta books, he significantly increased the amount of his reading.

Work steadily on building and maintaining classroom libraries. Classroom libraries need continuous attention. Weed out the books that are not moving, get copies of the hot new titles that all of your students want to read, and create displays that get your students' attention. Enlist your students' help in maintaining the library.

Independent-reading time is one of the components of workshop—yet another good reason for using a workshop framework. The most beneficial thing that your struggling readers can do during the school day is read. Give them time to read.

4. Provide in-class targeted instruction.

Intervention instruction is supplemental, *in addition* to regular classroom instruction. Provide every intervention student with small-group targeted instruction, at least four times a week in the regular classroom, delivered by the regular classroom teacher. Every day would be even better! Analyze assessment data, anecdotal notes, and work samples to determine the students' strengths and needs. Develop an instructional program that gives them an opportunity to use their strengths to bolster their needs.

Sandra made her small-group work with Kylie, Colin, and Blake a priority. She met with their group every day. Although word study was one of their primary instructional needs, they did not spend the entire group time on word study. They also applied the word study concepts to reading real books and writing.

Initially, Tara didn't much like the idea of teaching guided reading lessons to her fifth graders. However, Claire, the literacy coach, pointed out that these students were up to three years below the expected grade level and would benefit from explicit lessons on "how to read." Guided reading allowed Tara to closely observe her students while they were reading, coach them at the point of difficulty, and support them in developing effective and efficient reading strategies.

5. Provide time for teachers and interventionists to collaborate.

"If you could get all the people in an organization rowing in the same direction, you could dominate any industry, in any market, against any competition, at any time" (Lencioni, 2002, p. vii).

If teachers and interventionists would row in the same direction, it is quite likely that most students would need to spend considerably less time receiving intervention services. What does "rowing together" look like? There would be a coherent literacy curriculum in which the classroom teacher and the interventionist work toward the coordinated goals with their common students. Classroom teachers and interventionists would use the same language, the same anchor charts, and similar instructional materials.

How can we achieve "rowing together" in our schools? Teachers and interventionists need time to work together during the regular school day. If Claudia had known that Tyreese's class was learning about the civil rights movement, she probably wouldn't have focused on Ancient Egypt in the intervention room. If Marnie had had any idea that Liz was teaching a whole-class novel in the classroom, she would not have started another novel at the same time in the intervention room.

Even though Marnie and Liz were willing to work together, they had tremendous difficulty finding a time to meet. It is common practice for teachers and interventionists to schedule time to meet beyond the regular school day, but they shouldn't have to. In any other field, that would be unimaginable! Can you imagine a chef and sous chef having to meet at Starbucks before work to plan menus? How about the doctor and the nurse meeting after work in the hospital cafeteria to discuss patients' medications? It would never happen.

Administrators need to build in the time for teachers and interventionists to meet during the regular school day. Interventionists must participate in grade-level team meetings. If there are multiple interventionists in a school, focus their work on a two-grade-level span—three at the absolute most. Only one grade level would be even better. This would allow them to attend and actively participate in the grade-level team meetings. Coordinating instruction between the classroom and the intervention room would be a major focus.

Interventionists also need time to observe their students during regular instruction. The real measure of intervention instruction is how students apply it in the classroom and in the outside world.

Limiting interventionists to two or three grade levels and allocating time in their schedules to attend team meetings and observe intervention students during regular instruction would affect the number of intervention sessions offered each week and the number of intervention groups taught. These are hard choices. Schools often attempt to offer intervention classes to every single eligible student in the building. Once I observed an interventionist attempt to run an intervention group made up of 10 students. It is better to do a good job with fewer students than a marginal job with more students.

As far as fewer intervention class meetings for students goes, what you lack in quantity, you'll make up in quality. Intervention class sessions will be more effective because they are aligned with classroom instruction. The intervention class will be a true extension of the regular classroom. The students will greatly benefit from more cohesive instruction.

In the long history of our efforts to meet the needs of struggling learners, we have tried just about everything. We have tried special instructional materials, special instructional approaches, special classrooms, and even special schools. What we haven't tried often enough is

- using a workshop framework in the regular classroom that allows struggling learners to be actively engaged in learning all day using appropriate texts;
- providing targeted, in-class small-group instruction; and
- aligning classroom and intervention instruction.

If we can create schools that provide all three of these components, Monica might read happily ever after.

REFERENCES

Allen, J. (2000). *Yellow brick roads: Shared and guided paths to independent reading 4–12.* Portland, ME: Stenhouse.

Allington, R. L. (2011). *What really matters for struggling readers: Designing research-based programs.* (3rd ed.) Upper Saddle River, NJ: Pearson.

Allington, R. (2002, November). You can't learn much from books you can't read. *Educational Leadership,* 60 (3), 16–19.

Allington, R. L. (1977). If they don't read much, how they ever gonna get good? *Journal of Reading,* 21, 57–61.

Bear, D. R., Invernizzi, M. A., Templeton, S., & Johnaton, F. (2011). *Words their way: Word study for phonics, vocabulary and spelling instruction.* (5th ed.) Upper Saddle River, NJ: Pearson.

Brown, S. (2004). *Shared reading for grades 3 and beyond: Working it out together.* Wellington, NZ: Learning Media Limited.

Cunningham, A. E., & Stanovich, K. E. (1998). What reading does for the mind. *American Educator,* 1–8.

Dorn, L., & Soffos, C. (2011). *Interventions that work: A comprehensive intervention model for preventing reading failure in grades K–3.* Upper Saddle River, NJ: Pearson.

Fisher, D., Frey, N., & Lapp, D. (2008, April). Shared readings: Modeling comprehension, vocabulary, text structures, and text features for older readers. *Reading Teacher,* 6 (7), 548–556.

Fisher, D., Frey, N., & Lapp, D. (2012). *Text complexity: Raising rigor in reading.* Newark, DE: International Reading Association.

Lencioni, P. (2002) *The five dysfunctions of a team: A leadership fable.* San Francisco: Jossey-Bass.

Miles, K. H., Odden, A., Fermanich, M., & Archibald, S. (2004, Summer). Inside the black box: School district spending on professional development in education—lessons from five urban districts. *Journal of Educational Finance,* 30 (1), 1–26.

Richek, M. A., & McTeague, B. (1988). The "Curious George" strategy for students with reading problems. *The Reading Teacher,* 22, 220–226.

Routman, R. (2004). *Writing essentials: Raising expectations and results while simplifying teaching.* Portsmouth, NH: Heinemann.

Tovani, C. (2000). *I read it, but I don't get it: Comprehension strategies for adolescent readers.* Portland, ME: Stenhouse.

CHILDREN'S LITERATURE REFERENCES

Avi. (2005). *Poppy (Tales from Dimwood Forest).* New York: HarperCollins.

Betancourt, J. Pony Pals series. New York: Scholastic.

Bishop, N. (2010). *Lizards.* New York: Scholastic.

Blume, J. (1978). *Freckle juice.* New York: Yearling.

Boelts, M. (2009). *Those shoes.* Somerville, MA: Candlewick.

Bunting, E. *The wall.* (1992). New York: HMH Books for Young Readers.

Burnett, C., & Simmons, J. (1999). *Selma, Lord, Selma.* DVD. Burbank, CA: Walt Disney Home Entertainment.

Cabot, M. Allie Finkle's Rules for Girls series. New York: Scholastic.

Cebulash, M. (1993). *Willie's wonderful pet.* New York: Cartwheel Books.

Cleary, B. (1990). *The mouse and the motorcycle.* New York: HarperCollins.

Clements, A. (2006). *Things not seen.* New York: Penguin Group.

Creech, S. (2001). *Love that dog.* New York: HarperCollins.

Creech, S. (2010). *Hate that cat.* New York: HarperCollins.

Curtis, C. P. (2001). *The Watsons go to Birmingham—1963.* New York: Laurel Leaf.

DeGross, M. (1998). *Donovan's word jar*. New York: Harper Trophy.

Demi. (2001). *Gandhi*. New York: Margaret K. McElderry Books.

DiCamillo, K. (2009). *Because of Winn Dixie*. Somerville, MA: Candlewick.

Hiassen, C. (2005). *Hoot*. New York: Yearling Books.

Farshtey, G. The Bionicle series. New York: Papercutz.

Fleischman, P. (2004). *Seedfolks*. New York: Harper Trophy.

Garland, S. (1997). *The lotus seed*. New York: HMH Books for Young Readers.

Grimes, N. (2002). *Bronx masquerade*. New York: Speak.

Gutman, D. My Weird School series. New York: HarperCollins.

Heide, F. P. (1995). *The day of Ahmed's secret*. New York: HarperCollins.

Hughes, D. Angel Park All-Stars series. New York: Random House.

Ingalls Wilder, L. (2004). *Little house in the big woods*. New York: HarperCollins.

Kinney, J. (2007). *Diary of a wimpy kid*. New York: Amulet Books.

Kline, S. Horrible Harry series. New York: Puffin.

Kotsut, R. Lego City series. New York: Scholastic.

LeGuin, U. (2003). *Catwings*. New York: Scholastic.

NBC News Presents. (2008). *Let Freedom Ring*. DVD. New York.

Martin Jr., B. (1967). *Brown Bear, Brown Bear, what do you see?* New York: Henry Holt.

McDonald, M. (2010). *Judy Moody*. Somerville, MA: Candlewick.

McMullan, K. (1999). *Fluffy goes to school*. New York: Scholastic.

McMullan, K. (2001). *Fluffy's school bus adventure*. Scholastic.

McMullan, K. (2002). *Fluffy goes apple picking*. Scholastic.

Palcy, E. (2004) *Ruby Bridges*. DVD. Burbank, CA: Walt Disney Home Entertainment.

Park, B. (1997). *Skinnybones*. New York: Yearling.

Pilkey, D. (2000). *Ricky Ricotta's mighty robot*. New York: Scholastic.

Pilkey, D. (2000). *Ricky Ricotta's giant robot vs. the mutant mosquitos from Mercury*. New York.

Rappaport, D. (2001). *Martin's big words*. New York: Hyperion.

Riordan, R. Percy Jackson and the Olympians series. New York: Hyperion.

Roy, R. The A to Z Mystery series. New York: Random House.

Rylant, C. (1996). *Every living thing.* New York: Aladdin

Scieszka, J. (2004). *Tut, Tut.* New York: Puffin Books.

Scieszka, J. (1996). *The true story of the three little pigs.* New York: Puffin Books.

Seuss, Dr. (1961). *The Sneetches and Other Stories.* New York: Random House.

Seuss, Dr. (1971). *The Lorax.* New York: Random House.

Seuss, Dr. (1957). *The cat in the hat.* New York: Random House.

Spinelli, J. (1993). *Fourth grade rats.* New York: Scholastic Paperbacks.

Teague, M. (2002). *Dear Mrs. LaRue: Letters from obedience school.* New York: Scholastic.

Tripp, V. (1988). *Changes for Molly.* Middleton, WI: American Girl.

Turner, P. S. (2005). *Gorilla doctors: Saving endangered great apes.* New York: HMH Books.

Weston, C. The Diary of Melanie Martin series. New York: Yearling Books.

White, E. B. (2005). *Stuart Little.* New York: Harper & Row.

Wiseman, B. (1991). *Morris the moose.* New York: HarperCollins.

Woodson, J. (2004). *Locomotion.* New York: Speak.

Woodson, J. (2010). *Peace, locomotion.* New York: Puffin Books.

Yolen, J. Commander Toad series. New York: Puffin.